W9-ATP-811

CHALLENGE FOR SURVIVAL

CHALLENGE FOR
SURVIVAL

Land, air, and water
for man in megalopolis

EDITED BY

PIERRE DANSEREAU

with the assistance of

VIRGINIA A. WEADOCK

Foreword by William Campbell Steere

COLUMBIA UNIVERSITY PRESS
New York and London

ISBN: 0-231-03267-6
Library of Congress Catalogue Number: 78-98397
Printed in the United States of America

Sponsored by The New York Botanical Garden

9   8   7   6

CONTRIBUTORS

PIERRE DANSEREAU Institut d'Urbanisme, Faculté de l'Aménagement, Université de Montréal, Montréal, Québec, Canada

IAN MC HARG Department of Landscape Architecture, University of Pennsylvania, Philadelphia

BERNARD L. ORELL Weyerhaeuser Company, Tacoma, Washington

JEAN GOTTMANN School of Geography, University of Oxford, Oxford, England

AUGUST HECKSCHER Commissioner of Parks, New York, New York

PAUL BROOKS Houghton Mifflin Company, Boston, Massachusetts

BRUCE QUAYLE Sinclair Oil Corporation, New York, New York

FRANK E. EGLER Aton Forest, Norfolk, Connecticut

MILES P. SHANAHAN Sterling Forest Corporation, Tuxedo, New York

DAVID LOWENTHAL American Geographical Society, New York, New York

CHARLES C. MORRISON, JR. Director, New York State Natural Beauty Commission, Albany, New York

HELMUT E. LANDSBERG Institute of Fluid Dynamics and Applied Mathematics, University of Maryland, College Park

CHARLES F. LUCE Consolidated Edison Company, New York, New York

DAVID M. GATES Director, Missouri Botanical Garden; Department of Botany, Washington University, St. Louis, Missouri

CARL THOMPSON Environmental Health Unit, Hill and Knowlton, Inc., New York, New York

GEORGE M. WOODWELL Department of Biology, Brookhaven National Laboratory, Upton, New York

MATHEW M. SHAPIRO United Nuclear Corporation, Elmsford, New York

DIXY LEE RAY Pacific Science Center, Seattle, Washington

FRANKLIN S. FORSBERG Publisher, *Field and Stream,* Holt, Rinehart & Winston, New York, New York

RUTH PATRICK Department of Limnology, Academy of Natural Sciences of Philadelphia, Philadelphia, Pennsylvania

EDWARD R. TRAPNELL Consultant, The Ralph M. Parsons Company, Washington, D.C.

WILLIAM A. NIERING Director, Connecticut Arboretum; Department of Botany, Connecticut College, New London

SEYMOUR H. HUTNER Haskins Laboratories, New York, New York

EDMUND M. FENNER Department of Environmental Control, Johns-Manville Products Corporation, Manville, New Jersey

LEWIS MUMFORD Amenia, New York

FOREWORD

The extremely successful symposium, "Challenge for Survival/ 1968: Land, Air, and Water for Man in Megalopolis," presented by The New York Botanical Garden on April 25 at The Rockefeller University and on April 26 at the Botanical Garden, illustrates as well as any case history I can cite the evolution of an idea—and what is more important to us and our world today than ideas? As the first step in this evolution, our Native Plant Garden Committee, which has raised funds to endow an interesting and educational collection of native plants, proposed that some kind of symposium dedicated to an exchange of opinions and concepts of conservation of native plants would be useful. However, the larger scope of urban conservation was at once recognized by the administration, Board of Managers, and Women's Council of the Botanical Garden as having a much more immediate appeal and application. We are grateful to Mrs. Erastus Corning II, Chairman of the Women's Council, who served as chairman of the coordinating committee that first brought together and unified the many and diverse points of view concerning the Symposium. Also, through the Women's Council, she arranged the highly effective social events for the Symposium.

Just as the basic logistic arrangements did, the program itself evolved in a spectacular manner, thanks to the genius of Pierre Dansereau, a distinguished veteran of many national and international symposia (and at that time Senior Curator of Ecology at The New York Botanical Garden). At first conceived as a dialogue between professionals and advanced amateurs, the Symposium rapidly evolved into a three-way communication between representatives of science, government, and industry at all levels of specialization, so that the intelligent lay public and advanced amateurs had "equal time" with the professionals to present their viewpoints on problems of urban environment. During much of the program-planning stage, late in 1967 and early in 1968, Dr. Dansereau was in residence as Visiting Scholar at the Cranbrook Institute of Science, Bloomfield Hills, Michigan, on leave of absence from the Botanical Garden. Although questions of policy relating to the program were referred to him, many routine matters had to be settled and a vast amount of correspondence was handled at the Botanical Garden. Many individuals shouldered this task, and I would like to express my special thanks to Donald I. Selby, at that time Assistant Director for Public Affairs, for the time and energy that he and his staff put into this work, even though it sometimes meant that more central responsibilities had to suffer.

The National Science Foundation recognized the timeliness and value of our Symposium, one of the first to survey the total environmental problems of the largest urban area of the Western Hemisphere. We are deeply grateful to the National Science Foundation for a grant (GZ-777) to the Botanical Garden of $6,600 from its program of Public Understanding of Science to support some of the more scientific aspects of the Symposium. Even though the costs of the Symposium substantially exceeded income derived from registration fees and the NSF grant, the event was considered such an overwhelming success that The New York Botanical Garden was willing to meet this deficit. Even more, one of the most important results of the Symposium was the Botanical Garden's realization of the urgent need for a continuing series of such events. If we had experienced staff personnel who could devote full time to this activity, we would plan one or more symposia each year, but under present circumstances we look forward to an outstanding symposium in alternate years, with the main thrust on calling attention to problems of urban environment, and even more important, making positive and constructive recommendations for their solution.

To all the other individuals—staff members, members of the Board of Managers, and friends of the Botanical Garden at large— too numerous to mention by name here, who during the evolutionary stages served on planning committees, helped develop the program, and arranged logistic support, among many other essential activities, I express our warmest gratitude, both officially and personally. I am sure that Pierre Dansereau, in his Editor's Preface, will pay due and proper respect to those speakers and commentators who actually appeared on his program, and whose contributions appear in this volume.

William Campbell Steere
Executive Director

PREFACE

A science of human ecology is in the making. It has not found its bearings yet, for it remains dependent upon sociology and on human geography and has not nearly informed itself of the theoretical content of ecology.

A new discipline focused on the human habitat will hopefully emerge from a conversation between scientists and humanists trained in a variety of fields and well-grounded in one or more of them, but also open to the revelations their knowledge may bring to environmental processes. The implications of physics, molecular biology, biochemistry, evolution in weather, soil dynamics, plant and animal coexistence are all in need of re-examination after they have been tested by the newer techniques of information theory, of behavioral science, of economics, and of anthropology. Need I add that the crucible of semantics offers proof of our knowledge and of the global expression of environmental phenomena.

A conversation for many voices has been attempted in this book, and it will be heard primarily for its content. The choice of participants and topics is fairly self-explanatory. I have tried further justification in my introductory chapter. It will be seen from the authors' affiliations and professional connections that the spectrum is a wide one: physicists oriented to meteorology and to biology, plant-ecologists involved in land-use, water economy, and physiology of radiation, geographers turned to urban dynamics and the psychology of landscape perception, experimental biologist concerned with the indices and volumes of productivity. Such a concert could well have been dissonant had not all of these specialists used their professional competence primarily as a platform from which to observe the management of land, air, and water by urbanized man.

And it was on this ground that they could engage architects, planners, educationists, administrators as well as financiers and businessmen to obtain the feedback so essential to proper statements about our environment.

It was the purpose of The New York Botanical Garden, as one of the great educational and research institutions of megalopolis, to open an arena in its inner circle where such an engagement could be staged. The collaboration of The Rockefeller University was most valuable in drawing together the participants and the commentators as well as an exceptionally representative audience. Students and young scientists, members of various philanthropic societies, conservation organizations, professionals of education, business, industry, and finance all took an active part.

It is hoped, therefore, that the scholarly value and the information content of this book will also serve the purpose of an experiment in communication.

I wish to thank the participants for their valuable contribution and for the pains they have taken in preparing their texts for publication. Miss Virginia A. Weadock, who has helped me so unfailingly on earlier tasks, has been involved in all of the phases of the present work. She deserves full credit for meticulous attention to detail and for many useful suggestions to the authors.

I fondly hope that Dr. William C. Steere's resolution to make this the first of many participations of botanists in urban affairs will be implemented. In my newly assumed role as a teacher of Ecology in an Institute of Urbanism, I know the cost and the difficulties of passing over from the biological sciences to the sciences of man, and also the joy and the profit of the frequent return journeys. Many of us, in the years to come, will adopt this way-of-life and will feel very much at home in undertakings such as the one that lies recorded between the covers of this book.

Pierre Dansereau

CONTENTS

CHALLENGE FOR SURVIVAL

Megalopolis: resources and prospect PIERRE DANSEREAU

Environmental science made its appearance a few years ago on university calendars and in public administrations. New programs and curricula, new services and departments were set up under this label. It may seem to many observers that nothing new is being contemplated and that a mere play on words is being enacted in order to dignify (if not to rehabilitate) a tired discipline. The generation born to Science in the thirties may now witness with suspicion the purifying baptism of emerging disciplines and their confirmation rides on new bandwagons (mostly star-spangled), and is understandably reluctant to grant them autonomy. But when such emergences have truly rejuvenated the field by effecting an authentic breakthrough, they have brought about a shift in intellectual allegiances and a consequent move in disciplinary boundaries, which in turn have disturbed curricular and administrative patterns. In the last several decades, demography, nuclear physics, cybernetics, topology, molecular biology, radiobiology, ecosystem-ecology have reached that stage in self-realization at which they must claim full freedom to borrow from other sciences in their own way, at the expense of a temporary break with the tradition from which they have sprung.

Environmental biology—and indeed environmental science as a whole—*came out of ecology and can only maintain its validity by squaring its conceptual and operational work in an ecological frame.*

Ecology, in turn, was born of the contemplation of the natural environment, of the intent desire to understand not only the dependence but also the interrelatedness of living beings. It was a part of other sciences before it achieved full stature. But it kept right on feeding on the data offered by many disciplines. When it applied itself to the task of evaluating resources, it had much to offer and sought a new niche in the academy. It was able to influence substantially the growth of other sciences. But in turn it will have to be transformed and reformed and to seek a larger sphere in a more broadly conceived environmental science. This is now being recognized by some universities, and it is affecting their curriculum and organizational structure.

It therefore seems relevant to look back to times and places where and when new developments became possible, because the cultural environment was ready, and to men and institutions whose availability matched this maturity or readiness.

EMERGENCE OF DISCIPLINES

Two main traditions are interwoven in the scientific endeavor: the descriptive and the functional. The field (or legitimate object) of a descriptive science is circumscribed by the materials to be studied. Thus, botany considers plants, zoology animals, and mineralogy rocks. It is possible to go to great lengths of refinement and precision by submitting rocks, plants, and animals to the test of "sophisticated" techniques and still not leave the orbit of description. On the other hand, the functional disciplines concern themselves more directly with process. Physiology, genetics, engineering, meteorology, psychology have developed various means of inquiry into the metabolic and dynamic responses of minerals, plants, and animals to forces contained within themselves or operating from outside. The built-in controls that have resulted from successive pulses of natural selection have left the organisms with varying ranges of response to environmental stimuli.

The cumulative effects of the growing complexity of matter as witnessed in the successive steps of corpusculization, phyletization, and socialization (see Teilhard de Chardin 1959) liberate new forces at each turn of the evolutionary stream. Our growing intimacy with these processes permits an ever more accurate reading of the historical record and a sharpening focus for general theories of matter and of behavior.

The very apprehension of such complexity is not every scientist's cup-of-tea. The qualities of perception and the talents of translation necessary for the proper exercise of this kind of investigation are potentially numerous. And yet they occur in such lopsided combination in any given individual that they predispose each one to certain disciplines. The highly desirable self-knowledge (exemplarily advocated by Socrates) that would check in time a venture in an unsuitable field is to this day not very common, psychological orientation tests notwithstanding. Congenital inabilities and even sheer physiological weaknesses, such as a low mathematical skill or an aberrant eyesight, may stand in the way of a career already launched. Scientists no less than artists have set for themselves goals which they are not competent to reach. This failure is often redeemed by the way in which the game is played (the style of Buffon) or by discovery itself. Thus Darwin deplored his own ineptitude in mathematics (deBeer 1965), sensing a further dimension which he felt unable to grasp.

These questions are given an implicit answer in the academic division of labor that has resulted in the structure of faculties, the assignment of "chairs," and the designing of curricula. If a department of psychology develops a large program on the "function of memory," it may be no time before this pursuit becomes the central labor of its members. A retrospective of science shows up a number of episodes in which the tail wags the dog for a long while before the beast can regain its balance (in our time: "chromosome botany," phytosociology, molecular biology, nuclear physics). And this may well be a necessary happening.

The progress of science is due almost entirely to the capacity of a very few individuals to devise an imaginative projection that lies more or less in the trajectory of past experience, but for which no convincing *prima facie* argument can be made. Such is the origin of those unsettling breakthroughs that suddenly mobilize the scientific world. The new hypotheses can only be formulated, however, if the scientist's grasp of past experience is very secure and if his means of expression are adequate. The latter implies a minimum of artistry, yes, artistry. Watson (1968) has touched the nerve of discovery in a very graphic way in his memoir on the revelation of DNA structure. Hans Selye's (1964) "From dream to discovery" tells another story in a somewhat longer perspective and in a more thoughtful vein, as does Goldschmidt's (1960) autobiography. Subsequently we find Theodosius Dobzhansky (1967) possibly "dreaming dreams no mortal ever dared to dream before" in his golden maturity. It is from such witnesses that we can get our best clues to the past and cues for the present.

ECOLOGICAL PLEXUS

Thus it has come about that the sciences have emerged from Science (as Science had issued from Knowledge) under the double impact of discovery and of the need for methodological autonomy. Medicine had to free itself from the broader physics, or natural history; later, pharmacy had to emerge from botany; economics from history, and so on. Ecology happens to have been born of systematic biology and to have then drawn most of its substance from phytogeography and zoogeography. The early borrowings of ecology were also taken from geology, climatology, and pedology, a fact that cast its future course partly outside the field of biology. Alexander von Humboldt (1807) had already drawn this compass very boldly and recast much of contemporary knowledge in an environmental context.

Concurrently, the galloping progress of physiology and genetics (functional disciplines) far outstripped the position achieved by ecology. But to this day they do so without benefit of the feedbacks that would have invigorated their own growth. The extensive research on pigments and on hormones, for example, has yet to be related to the environments that provide both the raw materials (resources) and the stimuli that allow natural selection to operate.

Meanwhile, both genetics and ecology were given appropriate niches in the academy, although not, it must be said, in the professional schools. (Almost none of the current graduates of our medical or engineering faculties have had the benefit of any but an undergraduate approach to these disciplines.) On the other hand, Fisheries, Forestry, and Wildlife Management have installed ecology at their very core, whereas Agriculture has remained rather aloof. Consequently, the developing science of Conservation, until the early 1950s, got its bearings from the biologically oriented natural scientists, foresters, and wildlifers. Legislators, economists, engineers, and public health administrators, however, were bound to challenge the claims for preservation, reservation, and protection variously made by the conservationists. It needed a very strong influx of the social and economic sciences into the thinking of the conservationists before the next step could be taken. This finally came about, and some universities gave it recognition in their curricula and even in departmental structures. Refashioned under the banner of *resource administration*, the new School of Conservation applied ecological principles to the management of the humanized landscape. It drew some of its adepts from non-biological fields of study and work, and sent them out into the world capable of fulfilling brand new functions.

Thus, in the recent past, engineering projects, regional planning units, public health teams, professional and political conferences have drawn upon ecologically minded participants newly emerged from one of these schools or much influenced by them.

Nowadays no one will fail to acknowledge that land, water, and air pollution are specifically ecological problems. More recently, noise has been recognized as a mechanism that overstimulates or depresses energy output in urban ecosystems.

FEEDBACK

Recognition of the psychological dimension, no longer as an elusive "value" but as a lever in the environment, is one of the developments that draws attention to the ultimate reaches of ecology in our society. It had been foreshadowed, to some extent, by animal ecologists in their population studies of insects, fishes, birds, and mammals, to be sure, but by 1966 when Robert Ardrey's *The territorial imperative* and Konrad Lorenz' *On aggression* were written for the benefit of a large audience, the anthropologists, social psychologists, and economists had worked their way back to animal ecology rather than forward from it, partly casting aside the greater caution and tentativeness of earlier workers like Buitendijk and Tinbergen. The publication in 1968 of Desmond Morris' book *The naked ape* seems to mock the fear of anthropocentric projections which have lingered in our vocabulary ("sun-loving," "halophile," "information," "homing") even if they have been eliminated from our explicit thinking and we no longer need be so apologetic. This inhibition seems to have lessened as the fascination of analogous processes has taken hold and as we have cast some of the weight of our interest from the outside world to self-revelation.

Nothing has brought this about more dramatically than the human population explosion which we have been so long in identifying as the major threat to our survival. Population growth is both a cause and an effect of the changing environment and its technological improvements, and the considerations which follow are, of course, to be read against the background of menacing multiplication.

Although there are several good textbooks of plant ecology, of animal ecology, and a few that attempt to cover both and, almost as an afterthought, to include man, we do not seem to be ready for a total apprehension of the acquisitions of ecology. A formal recognition of a limited number of *laws*, encompassing the facts and processes of environmental structures and dynamics, is yet to come.[1] It seems that much ground still has to be cleared.

Most of the ecologists who are centrally located in the discipline at this time are intent upon analyzing (taking apart) one or more *ecosystems*. This is now considered the basic environmental unit. It has been defined variously from its early coinage by Tansley in 1935 to this day. Duvigneaud (1963) writes: "The ecosystem is a functional system which includes a community of living beings and their environment. It consists of phytocoenosis, zoocoenosis, microbiocoenosis, and mycocoenosis and of all the nutritional and chorological links that bind them and of climatotope and edaphotope." Billings (1964) puts it more tersely: "Ecosystem: energy-driven complex of a community of organisms and its controlling environment." My own definition (1967): "*An ecosystem is a more or less closed environmental unit where the resources of the site are cycled by a biomass consisting of plant and animal populations associated in mutually compatible processes.*"

There is some dispute as to the areal extent of ecosystems: a few drops of water in the sheath of an epiphytic bromeliad is an ecosystem? The Forest of Arden is an ecosystem? Ireland is an ecosystem? I personally am inclined to reject the first and the last and to select an order of magnitude that is large enough to claim relative autonomy and not too large to defy concrete mensuration and is also homogeneous in its resources and processes. However that may be, the usefulness of the concept is well established and has served the application of an ecological conceptual framework so widely that the term has been appro-

---

[1] I have attempted this myself, in a very tentative way, in 1956, 1957, 1962, and 1966 (in Darling and Milton 1966). But the preoccupations of most workers in the various fields involved do not run to such formulations, and they are not, at present, being commonly used (as in physics or mathematics) as new starting points or even as relays.

priated by anthropologists, architects, sociologists, and philosophers.

The simple model of an ecosystem shows green plants rooted in the soil and exposed to air: they are agents of *primary production* capable of tapping the resources of the environment by absorption, respiration, and photosynthesis and of transferring the sun's energy through various processes of elaboration, transport, differentiation, and storage. The *primary consumers*, insects, birds, and various other animals, unable to use solar energy directly, unable to synthesize certain substances (such as vitamins and vegetable proteins), ingest plant materials and in turn elaborate bone, muscle, blood, chitin, and so on, which will serve as food to *secondary consumers*, or carnivores, which in turn. . . . The fate of particles taken out of the inert part of the ecosystem and infused into the stream of the biomass is truly cyclic, since, at every stage, elimination, excretion, injury, shedding, and death return materials to the environment, some to be lost by radiation, evaporation, ablation, migration, and so on, some to be plowed back into air or soil, and there to be broken down (reduced) to newly assimilable states. The most important characteristics of any given ecosystem are: (*a*) the *potential productivity* of the resources *in situ* as variously liberated by climate, atmosphere, parent-rock, soil, and organisms; (*b*) the *interlocking pathways* of the elements that are being cycled, as well as the rate at which this is being effected; (*c*) the *peculiar requirements* and tolerances of the agents [2] by which this cycling is accomplished, through a variety of tapping mechanisms, and their resulting relative efficiency; (*d*) the quality and quantity of the resulting *reinvestment*.

The classic representation of the ecosystem is a pyramid with many producers, fewer consumers of the first order, and ultimately very few of the highest order. The many borrowings

---

[2] I have attempted elsewhere to define a limited number of *coenotypes*, that is, plants whose hereditary make-up commits them to a "way-of-life" insuring a peculiar utilization of resources.

from mathematics, economics, sociology, cybernetics which are implied in the vocabulary of ecosystem-ecology make it that much easier to project the concepts to human habitats and therefore to ecosystems where it is man and not an eagle or a lion that occupies the top of the spire.

For instance, a New England village community will extend over some acres of land where the basic resources are indigenous and liberated by the direct impact of climate upon parent-material (although nitrates from Chile and lime from a nearby community have been imported). The transformation of air and soil elements is accomplished by green plants once imported as seed from a more or less distant source and of exotic origin (such as wheat from the Eastern Mediterranean, corn from Mexico, potatoes and tomatoes from South America, beets from Europe, apples from the Caucasus), whereas sugar from the maple "bush," cranberries from the bog, and blueberries from the pine barren are the only indigenous food products. Additional foodstuffs are imported already processed, and sometimes from very far away: sugar, molasses, tea, coffee, chocolate. Much of the production of the land is further transformed by primary consumers: pigs, horses, cattle, sheep, fowl. These exotic animals yield labor, food, and clothing or household materials: milk, meat, fat, eggs, wool, leather, horn, feathers. Silk and cotton and other fibers will have to be imported to supplement wool, as will a number of ornaments, instruments, and tools needed for handi-work. Shelter can be constructed entirely from minerals and timber yielded by the ecosystem, although processed products (nails, glass, paint) will have to be imported. All carnivores other than man (and a few dogs and cats) have been eliminated from the ecosystem: wolves, bears, foxes, and even hawks are chased away from the role which they would play at the secondary consumer level. In order to account for the flow of resources in this (as in any other) ecosystem, the links of cooperation-competition have to be sighted at each level. In the hayfield the grasses and legumes compete for light-air-water-soil, but they also provide each other with nutrients (the legumes by their associated nitrogen-fixing, symbiotic micro-organisms), conserve water, cast shade, and restore soil fertility through their decomposing parts. The vertical movement of vegetable materials to the next level (food for fowl, cattle) is followed by lateral links such as the feeding of milk to pigs, who transform it into fat and meat, and of forage to horses and oxen, who transform it into labor.

It is, however, at the level of man that the number of these lateral links increases greatly and that their complexity exceeds that of the "natural" ecosystem. The flow of products upwards to man may involve no transformation from the primary production level (lettuce, tomatoes) or the secondary level (milk, eggs, meat); and yet a *processing* may be necessary (butter, cheese, bacon, blended and preserved or canned products). Moreover, a lateral transfer of energy may be effected by *services:* in return for processing or labor or skill, the equivalent of a tax on the consumable product is in order. (No matter, for our purpose, that currency has replaced barter or share-cropping!) These operations, of course, require the circulation of many commodities not originating *in situ:* tin, glass, paper, metal, and many instruments, vehicles, and implements not producible by the ecosystem. Over and above this, the flow of *information* from outside is bound to be considerable: the impact of education, learning, artistic and scientific endeavor all strongly orient the ecosystem as a whole. In a very material sense, what the human community *desires* is a matter of constant projection upon the cycling of resources, quite in the same way as the predaciousness of the eagle, the hunger of the lion, the restlessness of the buffalo, the migratory urge of the Canada goose.

MAN'S WORLD

"Man's role in changing the face of the earth" can be seen as an *escalation* in the course of which boundaries of ecosystems of increasing orders of magnitude were transcended. In a book bearing that title and published thirteen years ago (Thomas 1956), a vast panorama of man's effect on the natural balance of community structures was drawn. In this collection of scholarly essays, the emphasis was almost constantly on man as a disturbing agent. Ten years later, a symposium conceived in the same spirit had partly reversed this view and was, in fact, directed to the "Future Environments of North America" (Darling and Milton 1966). The issues of human ecology and of its proper definition, of its emergence as a legitimate discipline, were constantly raised. Going back to Malthus and Darwin and picking up many clues from the more recent statements of Paul Sears (1957) and Marston Bates (1964), we can observe that much attention was given to the pressures exerted upon natural resources by "values" of one kind and another. The psychological dimensions of space-designing must be recognized as equal in importance to water-availability, soil-fertility, and mineral supply. The religious and social barriers against use of the land or of one of its products (some ethnic groups do not consume the meat of cattle, others will not eat horsemeat, and others disdain mollusks), the possibly non-utilitarian origins of domestication (Isaac 1963), far from presenting an imponderable, are proper objects for ecological weighting and integration.

As it turns out, in our present society the overwhelming controls exerted by the industrial process extend so broadly that there are virtually no more rural areas in the nineteenth-century sense (and mood) of the term. And beyond mere economic forces lie the political decisions that release them.

For instance, the American Association for the Advancement of Science has received the report of a committee appointed "to study the uses of chemical and biological agents to modify the environment." This committee has had to consider "major and minor alterations of the environment." It seems difficult for a practicing ecologist, who has any knowledge of field conditions, to satisfy himself that some of the modifications of landscape in Viet Nam are not irreversible and are, in any sense of the word, minor. Clean agriculture, clean industry, clean urbanization, and

clean war are about as clean as our conscience as scientists if we
have not kept ourselves somewhat aware of what goes on. Even
death on the electric chair or on the gibbet and the burying of
waste in the deep sea or the icecap do not cancel out a question-
able purpose.

INSTITUTES OF ENVIRONMENTAL SCIENCE

The crying need for a "new science" of environmental study,
with ecology at its core and medicine at all of its outlets, is now
being met by a few institutions of higher learning. Legislation is
always behind the times: it is the grammar that must follow
general usage. The backwardness of the civil and criminal code
is often shared by theology, philosophy, and other classificatory
disciplines that strongly influence the academic community, not
only in its thinking, but, of course, in its structure. However,
those universities that are not mere diploma factories geared to
providing the people with what they obviously want, have always constructed ivory towers where the Individual, not the
System, reigns. Maybe the bugging of the ivory tower by industry and government has contributed to the achievement of a
larger audience for imaginative scientists. Pressure upon the
university from outside as well as from within may induce a
more daring participation not merely in community affairs but
also in the leadership which they alone can provide towards a
better understanding and therefore a more responsible control
of whole environments in the full complexity of their relationships.

What, then, is an institute of environmental science (under
whatever name) capable of doing?

It will draw its strength from a few leaders whom it would be
very misleading to call *generalists* merely because of their broad
vision of environmental problems or because they are conversant
with the findings of many disciplines. This indeed they must be,
and yet they can make very little of such borrowed knowledge
unless they are thoroughly grounded (and therefore *specialists*)

in one of the sciences that compose the panel of environmental science.

But these gifted coordinators must have something to ordain, and they are bound to collaborate with workers in several fields who are themselves specialists, and possibly narrow ones. The beaming of intellectual energy to a limited object, to the exclusion of all other considerations, is one of the prime conditions of every advance in knowledge. Some men and women are incapable *by temperament* of any contemplation but this narrow apprehension. The truly gifted make up in depth what they may lack in breadth, and by shifting their gaze, they develop range. John James Audubon, whose life's work explains nothing, nevertheless accounts for a great deal. He is in the grand encyclopedic tradition of those who give a definitive shape to the human image of the world. The creators of prototypes are also great men; whether they are called Buffon, Linnaeus, Dostoevsky, Modigliani, or Henry Ford, they give us new bearings. Others are specialists *by discipline;* possibly wary of their own tendency to speculate, they delve eagerly into observation and experimentation, submit themselves to an exclusive methodology, curb their wandering curiosity, and embrace what seem to be minor objectives in order to develop the equipment that greater ventures require. (Witness Alfred Kinsey, who monographed insects and thereby furbished a tool which he successfully used in his classic study of human sexuality.) Such men may or may not ever break out of the specialist phase and become generalists, but they are the only ones who can. The race that has issued from Lamarck, Humboldt, and Darwin has produced a few in each generation.

The above may be a simplified view, and many institutions and organizations will harbor some intermediate types, as well as a large number of indifferent, basically undeveloped workers-in-the-hive who are just "doing a job," and to whom intellectual achievement has long been subordinate to the attainment of a minimal social status. This does not go without dedication, to be sure, but the cogs-in-the-wheel and the members of the task force can make no impact. In this perspective, it almost looks as though character and culture outweighed knowledge, and as though the particular field of specialization did not matter. To a certain extent I am inclined to think so, provided, of course, that the leadership is imaginative and competent and that many nearly unrelated fields of specialization are represented.

How many fields? Which fields? I would say, ideally, at least one representative each of earth sciences, biological sciences, sciences of man, technology (or engineering), agriculture (or forestry or wildlife management), public administration (or public health), economics (or political science). If the University of Zenith cannot compete with the University of Winnemac, it remains that both have a job to do in environmental science. This job should be geared to the general objectives of the institution, of the community which it serves, and indeed to that very environment in which it operates: Iowa in the center of its cornfield and Pennsylvania amid the smokestacks. Historical, no less than geographical, conditioning will have cast a greater weight on one or another of the participating disciplines. The emergence at this time in North America of such institutes shows the shifting prevalence of oceanography, range ecology, city planning, landscape architecture, agriculture, and industrial development as the principal focus. It is to be hoped that such a diversity will maintain itself, for the achievement of unity of knowledge in environmental science should be permissible on whichever ground one has achieved the greatest strength. It is on such ground that a sense of reality and a feeling of relevance can best be rooted.

Many structural problems are posed by this projection of a new interdisciplinary undertaking. I can only plant a few beacons, and I will refrain from offering a blueprint.

In the existing institutes it has seemed useful to adopt the following two (and seemingly contradictory) procedures: to make the direction of the institute free of immediate departmental authority, its director being responsible to a dean, a provost, a vice-president; and to give almost all members of the team a departmental affiliation and at least half-time departmental responsibility. The two basic functions of this interdisciplinary organization are thereby best assured: the coordinators (very few in number) have a free hand and remain attuned to the general purpose at all times, and the collaborators are close to the wellsprings of their discipline and personally involved in its progress.

Together, the members of an institute of environmental science may strive for many goals. If their coordination is good and if they have the wholehearted support of their administration, they will not lose their feeling of relevance and responsibility. This will express itself through several channels. *Research* on land use, productivity, pollution, social attitudes, planning, no matter how specialized, will be kept in line with some previously stated objectives of crucial import to the regional community. In fact, it is almost indispensable to cause a convergence of the personnel's attention to the local manifestation of a general problem. An outstanding example of this kind of sharp focus on an interdisciplinary endeavor is the Glen Canyon study summarized by J. D. Jennings (1966). *Public communication* is another necessity: keeping the lines open not only with the world of science, but also with the decision-making local and regional political authorities, the social clubs, and other pressure groups. It hardly seems necessary to point out that good interpreters at this level are possibly rarer than good scientific specialists: science-writers and science-speakers who are versed in Madison Avenue techniques but not steeped in its philosophy and not given to throwing semantic nets.

Not least is the *integration of environmental studies in the university's curriculum*. In a plea for diversity and heterogeneity on the campus, which I would waste no opportunity to make, I have in mind the enhancement of the best talents and powers of the members of the institute. It should be allowable for some to devote virtually all of their energy to one function alone: administration, promotion, research, or teaching. It strikes me, however, that the majority of the research scientists just cannot remain alive without benefit of teaching. Many of us feel that, if our teaching is any good at all, we learn as much from our students as they do from us.[3]

Now that mere conservation has been outstripped, that the anger of the disfavored and the bewilderment of the overfed are fully exposed, a new consciousness of environment is born. The apocalyptic figure of famine is being painted on the narrowing walls of our space in ever more threatening colors (see Dumont and Rosier 1966). The poisoning of huge flocks of sheep by escaped biological-warfare substances and of children by toxic milk offer dramatic evidence of our lack of awareness and of the unreliability of our control. The universities and other institutions of higher learning are bound to respond by giving a platform in full sight to the objective and coordinated study of the total environment. Tomorrow we must be equipped with a literature, and hopefully with visible achievements that will reshape our landscape inside and out.

INDUSTRY ON THE CHESSBOARD

Communications between the ivory tower and the executive tower have not lost all undertones of ambiguity. Conversations very similar to those of Michelangelo and Galileo with their popes can still be heard. But the Nobels, Guggenheims, Fords, Rockefellers, and Gulbenkians, unlike the Medici, have set up buffering foundations. The state itself (for instance, in Canada and in the United States) has set up foundations which are legally exempt from the curse of political control in their day-to-day operations if not in their budgetary claims and justification. This does not mean that all goes well between men of thought and men of power, and the issues concerning environment illustrate this dramatically. Egler (1962) has described and documented this situation devastatingly well.

The play of pressures in democratic as well as authoritarian

[3] I have developed this idea more fully elsewhere, in an essay entitled "The barefoot scientist" (Dansereau 1963).

societies often results in something less than freedom of expression by the scientist on social and economic issues that call for his technical competence. A combination of subliminal persuasion, of brash advertisement, of dangling rewards for conformity, of pessimistic Hearstian propaganda has resulted in the definitive intimidation of a great number of scientists who have refused to be "involved" in "controversial" issues and have steered clear of "sensitive" areas (the "silent scientists" of Egler [1964] in the *Silent Spring* of Rachel Carson [1962]). If everyone were brave we could have formed no notion of courage. It is not astonishing that few voices had been heard in scientific circles some years ago to raise the question of industry's duty to curtail and remedy the pollution of land, air, and water; the duty of government to curb the abuse of natural resources and to control radiation hazards. Barry Commoner (1966) draws a vivid picture of the developing conscience of an increasing number of scientists as citizens. Such periodicals as the *Bulletin of the Atomic Scientists* (now in its twenty-fifth year) and *Scientist and Citizen* have exercised a healthy vigilance on social, economic, and political situations where the scientist has an especial call as a witness. The American Association for the Advancement of Science has devoted an increasing amount of time in its annual meetings and of space in its publication (*Science*) to these issues and has invited reflexion, participation, and action. The Canadian Peace Research Institute has also been instrumental in uncovering the links of international conflict and resource utilization.

In spite of the antagonisms referred to above, I hope there are few scientists today who view the predicament of our survival and the unwise administration of our resources in the light of a conflict between science and industry, the latter being abetted by technology. Although an occasional dramatic application of the anti-monopoly laws, such as the condemnation (in 1968) by the courts of three major pharmaceutical companies, obliges us to face the fact of conspiracy, it is not possible to reduce our major problem of self-evaluation to a simple Marxian conflict of classes. There is not much to choose among the abuse of economic power, the blackmail of labor unions, the withdrawal of some desperate or hedonistic young people, and other negative behavior of social groups who are only too often abetted by the indifference of the scientists and the complacency of a whole bourgeois society. A failure to exercise our imagination, a failure to avail ourselves of our rights runs down the whole social scale, even in the most democratic communities. A great weakening of motivation must have preceded tolerance of the Hoffas, the Charles van Dorens, the Dodds, the Adam Clayton Powells. It is the same lack of nerve that has tolerated the increase of noise, the invasion of privacy, the obtrusive advertising, and air-poisoning.

We live in an industrial society that was made possible by science. The naïve surprise of the apprentice-sorcerer scientists is often matched by the cynical exploitation of the entrepreneurs. But these two villains are not alone in the farce of our menaced environment. We are all murderers and we are all guilty of inattention to our brothers if we have either refused their services or failed to appeal to their competence or to their power. The subversion of hope and the condoning of corruption have largely come about through our lack of awareness of environment, society, and history. The link between ugliness, spoilage, pollution, and social injustice should be evident at this time. A reviewer in the *Times Literary Supplement* (London) for January 18, 1968, put it this way: "While the American cities steadily enact the real meanings of centuries of semantic games with words like 'freedom,' 'slavery' and 'emancipation,' played with hypocrisy wildly beyond the resources of the dictionary and the sociologists, there must still be people who want to understand the backlog which has precipitated the revolt." This, apropos of the Negro problem, which is really the White problem, which is really modern man's predicament and suicidal mania.

We no longer live in the days of Henry Ford. Not all industrialists and financiers are content to read the poor-man's philosophers and economists in the *Saturday Evening Post* and the

Reader's Digest; many of them are well acquainted with William H. McNeil, John Kenneth Galbraith, Herbert Marcuse, Kenneth Boulding, Bertrand Russell, Lewis Mumford, Jean-Paul Sartre, Edmund Wilson, André Malraux, and other major witnesses of our age and interpreters of "the meaning of the twentieth century." The exercises in collective self-revelation to which these contemporary thinkers invite us have a dramatic content for the leaders of industry, finance, and commerce. Certainly the main challenge which it presents resides in their power to direct environmental change since the levers of implementation are in their hands. But what is the sense of implementation now that the "managerial revolution" is in full swing? The answer is: partnership of industry and science. This is the response so exemplarily illustrated by the life of Thomas Alva Edison (see Josephson 1959), who was scientist-technologist-industrialist, a prototypic figure with a backbone as solid as Abraham Lincoln's and quite free of any Horatio Alger aura.

In a much-read essay, Jean-Jacques Servan-Schreiber (1967) elevates the collaboration of science and industry to the power of a major historical development. Even an anti-Gaullist European has many reasons to be critical of America and to fear "the American challenge," but this writer takes an extremely lucid view of the impact on all future civilizations which American industrial methodology is now making. His argument reaches far beyond "if-you-can't-beat-them-join-them" in his recognition of the superior level of civilization developed in America thanks to continued and diversified major investments in research. And not only in industrial research but also in pure scientific research.

In 1968, in spite of whatever blemishes are evident on the American cultural image, the free play of its scientific endeavor and the lively exchanges between science and society are its distinguishing mark.

A less obvious development is the creation of structures for the participation of underprivileged (or under-powered?) parties (workers, students, teachers, the poor) in the solution of their own problems. It is just possible that some European countries whose democratic conscience has not itched as publicly as America's will soon be one jump ahead on this issue.

THE MEGALOPOLITAN ENVIRONMENT

Nowhere should this be more in evidence than in the great urban agglomerations. The nineteenth-century Belgian poet Emile Verhaeren (1895) wrote despairingly of "les villes tentaculaires" and of their devouring effect on the dreamy Flanders fields; in the twenties Paul Cohen-Portheim (1930) seemed to condone the British philosophy of regretful acceptance of residence in sinful, ugly cities and refuge in lovely, cultivated (and virtuous?) countryside (Thomas Hardy notwithstanding?). Such reactionary pastoral longings cannot well be programmed into our future, and the new look which we are casting at our cities is more hopeful. May the dogged and unrewarded optimism of Geddes, Le Corbusier, Frank Lloyd Wright stand us in good stead.

Peter Hall (1966), in his study of seven of the world's largest agglomerations, can find no evidence of a built-in mechanism that will eventually arrest either absolute or relative growth and no signal success in the efforts to do so artificially. This is one of the many facts of life with which contemporary man must cope. Looking back to the descriptions given by Eugène Sue and Dickens a century ago, we have reason for pessimism. Those who take comfort in a fundamentalist interpretation of the maxim that "the poor will always be with us" are playing a very dangerous game—at the risk of their own survival (Silone 1968).

Where does hope come from? Certainly there are many sources in the contemporary world: from the diversity of Oriental, African, and Occidental cultures, the wisdom of the Chinese, the pride of the Spaniards, the joy of the Bantus. Whereas some ethnic developments express themselves artistically, in poetry, literature, music, dance, or sculpture, there are just as signal successes in many social experiments and structures of tribal magnitude. In other words, the "wealth of the nations" can more readily be tapped by Everyman today than at any time in the past.

But my immediate concern is not with the much-needed improvement of our individual and collective motivation, but the convergence of our designs on the urban milieu. I have considerable hope in an intensified exchange of views between the scientists whose imaginary projections can reshape and sanify our environment and the industrialists who will not merely consent to change but will implement it and contribute to its planning.

First comes the matter of *definition*. Jean Gottmann's now classic work *Megalopolis* (1961), in a daring synthesis, has created a new framework for urban studies. This magnified pattern of human habitat is daily radiating information that controls human populations in the remotest corners. Its internal metabolism, its potential for change and renewal, the fluctuation ratios of its transformation of imported resources into creative exports invites a rigorous harnessing of scientific methodology for analysis. Doxiadis and his associates (1966) have directed the entire arsenal of such an analysis to the greater Detroit area. They define *ekistics* as ". . . the science . . . which conceives the human settlement as a living organism with its own laws and develops the interdisciplinary approach for solving its problems." But when they go on to say that its ". . . principal concerns are: creation of the most satisfactory environment for human activities" and ". . . selection of the most efficient means of creating this environment in a given local, regional, national or international setting," they set themselves up as the practitioners of a high art comparable to medicine. In fact, their second volume is entirely devoted to prediction of a kind which is only allowable in full knowledge of realistic alternatives, and can only be encompassed by a well-nourished scientific imagination.

I have said elsewhere (1966) (and have certainly echoed greater voices than mine) that all of our founderings are failures of the imagination, and I can only think that the awful and awesome perspectives that we have opened for ourselves in the atomic and space age, and that the new magnitude of disaster which we have made possible, can only be countered by our

ability to think in purely futuristic terms and not by constructing
the mosaic of things-to-come out of worn pieces from the past.
Paul Valéry (1936) put this more elegantly, at the turn of the
century, when American aggression against Spain made him think
of himself for the first time as a European and wonder what
Europe would be, indeed *if* it would be. Some forty years later
the European will for unity is half positive and half self-defen-
sive.

We place our hope, therefore, in the clear vision of our scientists and in the strong will of our industrialists. The probe of
analysis must sink deeply into the environment in which we are
plunged; our enquiry can be shackled by no interests and no
values other than the unveiling of the natural universe and our
exploitation of its resources and harnessing of its processes. The
heartbreaking images of poverty, hunger, spoilage, ugliness, and
degradation must all be flashed at once on the multiple screens
which expose our modern sensibility to pain, anger, and delight.
We cannot abolish the fear upon which bourgeois morality is
based (and on what else do Soviet and Maoist ethics rest?). But
the violent climate of our days may well exorcize the personal
possessiveness, the main obstacle to harmony and collective progress, in a spirit of sharing.

The partnership of industry and science is essentially a going
concern in North America. It is heartening to witness not only
the development of scientific laboratories and colloquia in many
of the large industrial emporia where the boundary between pure
and applied research (or should I say "mission-oriented" research?) has been quietly allowed to dissolve, but also the emergence of teams of scientists, engineers, and administrators (most
of whom would be qualified to teach in a university or to function
as business executives) operating variously as consultants, planners, and implementers of minor and often major works. The
emergence of this third force, as it were, upon which governments unload large responsibilities, and upon which financial
pressures are not overly binding, presents a strong element of

diversification and opportunity for new options. This is one of the outstanding characteristics of a more mature society.

The rising force of managerial control is not without its pitfalls, admittedly. The abuse of hidden persuasion, the debasement of some of our values, the myopic concentration on immediate objectives, not to mention unthinking activism and sheer entrepreneurship, are all within sight. Nor has the welfare state developed social and psychological apparatus equal to its economic implementation. Ignazio Silone (1968), in a thoughtful recapitulative essay, offers us some disenchanted views of the unevenness of this correction of economic unbalance. But some of those who can be held responsible for education reflect the mirror-image of this decadence in a slackening purpose, by showing a hand that holds the keys of knowledge too loosely, by living in unpardonably shabby academic communities, by absconding in the refuges of sheer verbal gargle, and by their refusal of involvement.

The new society that is truly fit to meet the "challenge for survival" needs more than ever before a sharply-focused network of communication. McLuhan's repeated message (1964) has hopefully massaged rather than brainwashed us into "understanding media" and breaking out of the passive mood which some of them seem to have induced. The last page of *The medium is the massage* (McLuhan and Fiore 1967) offers a detached quotation from Alfred North Whitehead: "It is the business of the future to be dangerous." We can only accept this restatement of the Nietzschean inducement.

A PLAN FOR A DIALOGUE

The identification of these dangers, the not always obvious connections between them, and also their nature as the obverse of the great benefits of modern civilization are the very stuff of the many discussions that are currently taking place on the shaping of the human environment. I cannot hope to summarize the considerable body of thought and to evoke the many images which have been drawn as prime examples of the escalated force of man and of his impact, proximate and remote, upon his habitat. Eldridge (1967) has edited a very rich collection of essays, nearly 1200 pages, which look into the various aspects of "taming megalopolis." A review of this work would look like a *status questionis* of the magnitude of our ills and of the weakness of our aims.

No understanding of the expanded and still permeating noösphere is quite possible without due consideration of *ultimate concern* as a polar attraction. It is not my purpose, in the present context, to consider man's destiny or man's fate and to situate the present inquiry in a perspective such as Teilhard de Chardin (1959) offers us, and such as Theodosius Dobzhansky (1967) has outlined. I had rather stop short of this point of high convergence, although I am aware that many of the leads from scientists and industrialists can only tend in that direction and that many of their questions can only be answered in these terms. The quality of environment is the matrix of human happiness and fulfillment.

It is therefore proposed to plunge back to the old pagan concept of nature and to consider, within the confines of megalopolis, the human population in its relation to the vital elements: land, air, and water. As for fire, it is possibly even more pervasive and inevitably flashes through. Such a recourse to primeval elements responds to a singularly modern sensibility. One of the great philosophers of our time has structured a post-Freudian *summa* upon them: Gaston Bachelard has entitled four of his books *L'eau et les rêves, L'air et les songes, La terre et les rêveries de la volonté, La psychanalyse du feu.*

The more modest endeavor we have in mind will consist in appraisals of the natural mechanics of the elements in renewal and self-exploitation, through tapping by plants and animals and under human management. Such a survey need not involve a full recapitulation of the mutations in the landscape that produced its residual resources (for example, Manhattan's recovery

from the Wisconsin glaciation and subsequent development of
soils and vegetation variously exploited, transformed, replaced,
and stamped out by urbanization). It is set, nevertheless, in an
ecological perspective, and the changing values of the land,
quality of the air, and uses of the water will be considered as
entering one or more of the cycles that activate the ecosystem.

Land. The reshaping of landscape from its primeval through its
agricultural and industrial phases as can be witnessed on the
edges of megalopolis gives us some of our bearings. On the one
hand, it recapitulates some of the steps that led to the "asphalt
jungle," whereas on the other hand the modern suburb and exurb
are recent phenomena with unprecedented requirements. The
new and often dangerous biochemical and biological controls
encounter here their most crucial test and their most signal success.

The acquisition of land for protection and limited productivity
as urban forest or parkland, or indeed as nature preserve, is geared
to a concept of citizenship and a measure of decentralized responsibility that requires a delicate balance and can often endanger the democratic process. Entrenched privilege can only
too readily put on the mask of esthetic and scientific preservation. Granted that the *chasse gardée* of the wealthy of 1850 to
1950 has saved the Gaspé salmon and the Westchester hard-
woods, we cannot allow public trusteeship to be a mere screen
for enduring privilege, and we must also question a shift in tenure
that would turn all wild land to recreation uses.

The kind of planning needed for greenbelts to circle the denser
agglomerations and penetrate to their blackest centers seems to
require the towering influence of men like John Muir, Frederick
L. Olmsted, Oswaldo Cruz, and Baron Haussmann whose knowledge of popular myths and dedication to the *res publica* were
bolstered by a prophetic view and solid grasp of reality. However, the swing of a liberal economy and the play of popular will
continue to make a pawn of green areas.

The peculiar conjuncture of tenure, management, and administration in urban and industrialized areas and in the rise or fall of economic potential within their immediate orbit severely limits the power of the resident and of the commuting population to stamp its values upon the landscape. A shift in priorities for development and transformation (beautification, trafficability, zoning, for example) is almost always at hand. The role of local groups, involving a well-informed and participating citizenry, will always remain of prime importance. But no long-range assignment in a rapidly changing landscape is possible without broad regional (or even state or national) planning.

Air. The gravitation and rotation of our planet condition the displacement of air masses, and the continental blocks at various latitudes determine a regime that has fluctuated severely through time. The intercepting and perturbing effect of urban areas with their radiation of heat and stagnation of fumes must be seen essentially as a modification of a regional pattern of heat and precipitation. The sharply defined layering of vari-colored air in the canyons of New York City offers many microclimates each with its load of poisons. But the natural flushing that breaks the stratification cannot be depended upon. . . .

Plants very conveniently signal the changes in environment. It is the prime business of the ecologist to detect indicator species. Thus, lichens are highly sensitive to polluted air (LeBlanc 1961), and actually offer a reliable gamut of responses that permits a gauging of degrees of toxicity. This inferential approach is now complemented by a series of biophysical measurements that tap the pulse of exchange between environment and organism (Gates 1962) at their ultimate point of contact. We cannot hope to understand the effects of pesticides and pollutants until our picture of these gateways has been considerably sharpened.

The entry into the organism of radioactive particles presents something more than a singular instance of toxicity. The problems of emission (natural and artificial), of transport and fallout, are closely tied with the dynamics of climate and microclimate, but the tissular, cytological, and molecular effects require a totally different technical approach. Fortunately, a new generation of workers is qualifying for this task (Woodwell 1965).

To breathe freely and to catch one's breath have several meanings beyond the inhaling of a minimum quantity of oxygen. "Open air" is a myth as well as a physiological need. And the shaping of our cities, the pruning of our hedges, the plantings in our parks are not merely a cleansing operation. The play of cultural imagery (Huth 1957) is a powerful agent in the design of the landscape and the purpose of conservation. A renewed interest in this approach to man's environment (Lowenthal 1964, Glacken 1966) is giving rise to ethno-science (Sturtevant 1964) and ultimately to ethno-ecology (Dansereau 1969).

Water. The questions raised about the nature of air and land resources, their origin, their renewability, their mode of utilization by plants, animals, man, and the changing (and often culturally determined) attitudes of man towards them, equally apply to water.

The wetlands offer an especially favorable background upon which to rehearse all of these issues (Niering 1966). The remaining saltmarshes that grace the eastern periphery of the Washington–New York–Boston megalopolis, with their inner estuarian fringes of marsh, swamp, and bog, have recently been the theatre of heated debates where scientific, aesthetic, historical, and economic values have been diversely weighted. This controversy should have been most enlightening, since it served the purpose of a better definition of the values implied and put a price on the stakes. It is precisely such a public hearing that will lead to a truly free choice.

Limnology has developed an increasingly satisfactory methodology which has admirably served the growing purposes of productivity measurement (Hutchinson 1957, 1966). It has also been applied to the test and classification of pollution, industrial and otherwise. The Hudson River, mapped according to these criteria, is a sorry sight. And Lake Erie has been called a cesspool.

It is not too difficult to retrace the origins of this spoilage, although we have not envisaged nearly all of its effects and even less considered the large-scale operations which could reverse the process where that is still possible. Some examples, fortunately, can be adduced as proof of adequate technical knowledge and equipment on the one hand and of the awakening of social conscience on the other.

Actually, botanical gardens and specialized research laboratories are hard at work in the intersecting areas of water productivity and pollution. Protozoa in the water (as lichens on land) are "toxicological tools" (Hutner 1964). The future of plankton and algae may loom very large in the history of our species. The technical problems of protection of their habitat, of stimulation of their growth are paralleled by much less explored questions of processing for food or industrial materials and last but not least the psychological and cultural dimensions of their acceptability to various human groups.

CONCLUSION

This proposed review of man's environment ranges widely. It suggests, as an image, the small figure of a South Sea Islander, with bare feet clasping the edge of a coral reef, throwing a fine-textured net into the sea. The multicolored catch brings wanted and unwanted objects, and it does not sample the whole world that lies below his sight in the mirrored sea. The castings of science are not all that blind, to be sure, but its findings are sometimes equally surprising and the serendipitous happenings are often the scientists' most cherished reward.

What is being attempted here is a mere blazing of a trail, with rather conspicuous *points de repère*, on the land, in the atmosphere, and in the waters. The theme which hopefully runs through this discourse for many voices is the desire of man to learn through deference to natural facts and his will to survive by disciplining himself to a wise use of his resources, including the unruly forces of his mind and emotions. "When not curbed by hostile environmental pressures, man's elaboration of symbolic culture answered a more imperative need than that for control over the environment—and, one must infer, largely predated it and outpaced it," writes Lewis Mumford (1967), reflecting upon the early consciousness and implicit motivation of an emerging technology.

Anthropological and sociological research, permeated by the Freudian and post-Freudian unveiling of motivation, give us a renewed insight of "the city in history" (from Fustel de Coulanges to Lewis Mumford), and are providing us with a new language to set our values in perspective.

Thus, more conversations must take place in the ivory tower between those of us who emerge from our struggles with the land, the atmosphere, and the water and those who probe the visceral and cerebral anguishes of man. Knowledge and consciousness have determined our wanderings in history and the complex sado-masochistic game of social stratification and economic flow. Our world in all its parts is perilously power-conscious, but it has an unprecedented opportunity to make enlightened decisions. This happy state rests upon the developing harmonious intercourse of science and society.

REFERENCES

Ardrey, Robert. 1966. *The territorial imperative.* New York, Atheneum, xiv + 390 pp.

Bates, Marston. 1964. *Man in nature*, 2nd edition. Englewood Cliffs, N.J., Prentice-Hall Company, Inc., x + 116 pp.

Beer, Sir Gavin de. 1965. *Charles Darwin: a scientific biography.* New York, Natural History Library, xx + 295 pp.

Billings, W. D. 1964. *Plants and the ecosystem.* Belmont, California, Wadsworth Publishing Company, v + 154 pp.

Carson, Rachel. 1962. *Silent spring.* Boston, Houghton Mifflin Company, xiii + 368 pp.

Cohen-Portheim, Paul. 1930. *England, the unknown isle.* London, Duckworth Company, 237 pp.

Commoner, Barry. 1966. *Science and survival.* New York, Viking Press, 150 pp.

Dansereau, Pierre. 1956. Le régime climatique régional de la végétation et les contrôles édaphiques. *Rev. Can. Biol.* 15(1):1–71.

Dansereau, Pierre. 1957. *Biogeography: an ecological perspective.* New York, Ronald Press Company, xiii + 394 pp.

Dansereau, Pierre. 1962. An application of ecological laws to woodlots. *Connecticut Agr. Exp. Sta. Bull.* 652:45–56; *Sarracenia* 7 (1962), 14 pp.

Dansereau, Pierre. 1963. The barefoot scientist. *Colorado Quarterly* 12(2):101–115. (Also: *Inst. Arctic & Alpine Research, Contrib.* 10: 101–115.)

Dansereau, Pierre. 1966. Ecological impact and human ecology. In Darling and Milton, pp. 425–462.

Dansereau, Pierre. 1967. The post-conservation period: a new synthesis of environmental science. *Cranbrook Inst. Sci. News Letter* 37(4):42–49.

Dansereau, Pierre. 1969. *Ecological impact.* London, Penguin Books (in preparation).

Darling, F. Fraser, and John P. Milton (eds). 1966. *Future environments of North America.* New York, Natural History Press, xv + 767 pp.

Dobzhansky, Theodosius. 1967. *The biology of ultimate concern.* New York, New American Library, xviii + 152 pp. (See also Bentley Glass' review in *Scientific American* (1968) 218(2): 133–136.)

Doxiadis, Constantinos A. 1966. *Emergence and growth of an urban region: the developing urban Detroit area.* Detroit, Detroit Edison Company. Volume I: *Analysis,* xx + 335 pp. Volume II: *Future alternatives,* xxxii + 408 pp.

Dumont, René, et Bernard Rosier. 1966. *Nous allons à la famine.* Paris, Editions du Seuil, 280 pp.

Duvigneaud, Paul. 1963. *L'écologie, science moderne de synthèse.* Volume 2: *Ecosystèmes et biosphère.* Bruxelles, Minist. Educ. Nat. et Cult., Documentation 23, 130 pp.

Egler, Frank E. 1962. On American problems in the communication of biologic knowledge to society. *Dodonaea* 30:263–304.

Egler, Frank E. 1964. Pesticides—in our ecosystem. *American Scientist* 52(1):110–136.

Eldridge, H. Wentworth (ed.). 1967. *Taming megalopolis*. New York, Anchor Books, Doubleday and Company, Inc., Volume I: *What is and what could be*, xv + 576 pp. + index. Volume II: *How to manage an urbanized world*, ix + 577–1168 + index.

Gates, David M. 1962. *Energy exchange in the biosphere*. New York, Harper & Row, viii + 151 pp.

Glacken, Clarence. 1966. Reflections on the man-nature theme as a subject for study. In Darling and Milton, pp. 355–371.

Goldschmidt, Richard B. 1960. *In and out of the ivory tower: the autobiography of Richard B. Goldschmidt*. Seattle, University of Washington Press, xiii + 352 pp.

Gottmann, Jean. 1961. *Megalopolis: the urbanized northeastern seaboard of the United States*. New York, Twentieth Century Fund, xi + 810 pp.

Hall, Peter. 1966. *The world cities*. New York, McGraw-Hill Book Company, 256 pp.

Humboldt, Alexander von. 1807. *Essai sur la géographie des plantes*. Paris, Levrault, Schoell; Sherborn Fund Facsimile 1 (British Museum, London, 1959), pp. xxxv + 153–155.

Hutchinson, G. Evelyn. 1957. *A treatise on limnology*. Volume I. New York, John Wiley & Sons, v + 978 pp.

Hutchinson, G. Evelyn. 1966. *A treatise on limnology*. Volume II. New York, John Wiley & Sons.

Huth, Hans. 1957. *Nature and the American: three centuries of changing attitudes*. Berkeley, University of California Press, xvii + 250 pp.

Hutner, Seymour H. 1964. Protozoa as toxicological tools. *Jour. Protozool.* 11(1):1–6.

Isaac, Erich. 1963. Mythes, culture et élevage. *Diogène* 41:72–95.

Jennings, J. D. 1966. *Glen Canyon: a summary*. Salt Lake City, University of Utah Press, University of Utah Anthropological Papers, No. 81, vii + 84 pp.

Josephson, Matthew. 1959. *Edison, a biography*. New York, Mc-Graw-Hill Book Company, xii + 511 pp.

LeBlanc, Fabius. 1961. Influence de l'atmosphère polluée des grandes agglomérations urbaines sur les épiphytes corticoles. *Rev. Can. Biol.* 20:823–827.

Lorenz, Konrad. 1966. *On aggression*. New York, Harcourt, Brace & World, xiv + 306 pp.

Lowenthal, David. 1964. Is wilderness 'paradise enow'? Image of nature in America. *Columbia University Forum* 7(2):34–40.

McLuhan, Marshall. 1964. *Understanding media: the extensions of man*. New York, McGraw-Hill Book Company, vii + 359 pp.

McLuhan, Marshall, and Quentin Fiore. 1967. *The medium is the massage*. New York, Bantam Books, 160 pp.

Morris, Desmond. 1968. *The naked ape*. New York, McGraw-Hill Book Company, 252 pp.

Mumford, Lewis. 1967. *The myth of the machine: technics and human development*. New York, Harcourt, Brace & World, 342 pp.

Niering, William A. 1966. *The life of the marsh*. New York, McGraw-Hill Book Company, 232 pp.

Sears, Paul B. 1957. *The ecology of man*. Eugene, Oregon, Condon Lectures, Oregon State System of Higher Education, 61 pp.

Selye, Hans. 1964. *From dream to discovery*. New York, McGraw-Hill Book Company, xiv + 419 pp.

Servan-Schreiber, Jean-Jacques. 1967. *Le défi américain*. Paris, Denoël, 342 pp. (English translation, 1968, *The American challenge*.)

Silone, Ignazio. 1968. Re-thinking progress. *Encounter* 30(3):3–12; (4):27–40.

Sturtevant, William C. 1964. Studies in ethno-science. In *Transcultural studies in cognition*, ed. by A. K. Romney and R. G. D'Andrade, *American Anthropologist* (Spec. Publ.) 66(3:pt.2): 99–131.

Tansley, A. G. 1935. The use and abuse of vegetational concepts and terms. *Ecology* 16(3):287–307.

Teilhard de Chardin, Pierre. (1955) 1959. *The phenomenon of man*. New York, Harper and Row, 320 pp.

Teilhard de Chardin, Pierre. (1959) 1964. *The future of man*. New York, Harper and Row, 319 pp.

Thomas, William L., Jr. (ed.). 1956. *Man's role in changing the face of the earth*. Chicago, University of Chicago Press, xxxviii + 1193 pp.

Valéry, Paul. 1936. *Regards sur le monde actuel*. Paris, Librairie Stock, 214 pp.

Verhaeren, Emile. 1895. Les villes tentaculaires. In *Oeuvres Complètes* (1923). Volume I, pp. 95–202. Paris, Mercure de France.

Watson, James D. 1968. *The double helix.* New York, Atheneum, xvi + 237 pp.

Woodwell, George M. (ed.). 1965. *Ecological effects of nuclear war.* Upton, New York, Brookhaven Natl. Lab., Biol. Dept. BNL 917 (C–43), v + 72 pp.

Photo by Walter Singer: A section of the natural forest
in The New York Botanical Garden, Bronx, New York.

LAND

The place of nature in the city of man IAN L. McHARG

Before we convert our rocks and rills and templed hills into one spreading mass of low grade urban tissue, under the delusion that, because we accomplish this degradation with the aid of bulldozers and atomic piles and electronic computers, we are advancing civilization, we might ask what all this implies in terms of the historic nature of man.—LEWIS MUMFORD (1956).

The subject of this essay is an inquiry into the place of nature in the city of man. The inquiry is neither ironic nor facetious but of the utmost urgency and seriousness. Today it is necessary to justify the presence of nature in the city of man; the burden of proof lies with nature, or so it seems. Look at the modern city, that most human of all environments, observe what image of nature exists there—precious little indeed, and that beleaguered, succumbing to slow attrition.

William Penn effectively said: Let us build a fair city between two noble rivers; let there be five noble squares, let each house have a fine garden, and let us reserve territories for farming. But that was before rivers were discovered to be convenient repositories for sewage, parks the best locus for expressways, squares the appropriate sites for public monuments, farm land best suited

Reprinted from *The Annals of the American Academy of Political and Social Science*, Volume 352, March, 1964; lightly edited.

for buildings, and small parks best transformed into asphalted, fenced playgrounds.

Charles Eliot once said, in essence: This is our city, these are our hills, these are our rivers, these our beaches, these our farms and forests. I will make a plan to cherish this beauty and wealth for all those who do or will live here. And the plan was good but largely disdained. So here, as elsewhere, man assaulted nature disinterestedly, man assaulted man with the city; nature in the city remains precariously as the residue of accident, rare acts of personal conscience, or rarer testimony to municipal wisdom, the subject of continuous assault and attrition while the countryside recedes before the annular rings of suburbanization, unresponsive to any perception beyond simple economic determinism.

Once upon a time, nature lay outside the city gates a fair prospect from the city walls, but no longer. Climb the highest office tower in the city, when atmospheric pollution is only normal, and nature may be seen as a green rim on the horizon. But this is hardly a common condition, and so nature lies outside of workaday experience for most urban people.

Long ago, homes were built in the country and remained rural during the lives of persons and generations. Not so today, when a country house of yesterday is within the rural–urban fringe today, in a suburb tomorrow, and in a renewal area of the not-too-distant future.

When the basis for wealth lay in the heart of the land and the farms upon it, then the valleys were verdant and beautiful, the farmer steward of the landscape. But that was before the American dream of a single house on a quarter acre, the automobile, crop surpluses, and the discovery that a farmer could profit more by selling land than crops.

Once men in simple cabins saw only wild nature, silent, implacable, lonely. They cut down the forests to banish Indians, animals, and shadows. Today, Indians, animals, and forests have gone, and wild nature, silence, and solitude are hard to find.

When a man's experience was limited by his home, village, and environs, he lived with his handiworks. Today, the automobile permits temporary escapes from urban squalor, and suburbanization gives the illusion of permanent escape.

Once upon a time, when primeval forests covered Pennsylvania, its original inhabitants experienced a north temperate climate, but, when the forests were felled, the climate became, in summer, intemperately hot and humid.

Long ago, floods were described as Acts of God. Today, these are known quite often to be consequences of the acts of man. As long ago, droughts were thought to be Acts of God, too, but these, it is now known, are exacerbated by the acts of man.

In times past, pure air and clean abundant water were commonplaces. Today, "pollution" is the word most often associated with the word "atmosphere," drinking water is often a dilute soup of dead bacteria in a chlorine solution, and the only peoples who enjoy pure air and clean water are rural societies who do not recognize them for the luxuries they are.

Not more than two hundred years ago, the city existed in a surround of farm land, the sustenance of the city. The farmers tended the lands which were the garden of the city. Now, the finest crops are abject fruits compared to the land values created by the most scabrous housing, and the farms are defenseless.

In days gone by, marshes were lonely and wild, the habitat of duck and goose, heron and egret, muskrat and beaver, but that was before marshes became the prime sites for incinerator wastes, rubbish, and garbage—marshes are made to be filled, it is said.

When growth was slow and people spent a lifetime on a single place, the floodplains were known and left unbuilt. But, now, who knows the floodplain? *Caveat emptor.*

Forests and woodlands once had their own justification as sources of timber and game, but second-growth timber has little value today, and the game has long fled. Who will defend forests and woods?

Once upon a time, the shad in hundreds of thousands ran

strong up the river to the city. But, today, when they do so, there is no oxygen, and their bodies are cast upon the shores.

THE MODERN METROPOLIS

Today, the modern metropolis covers thousands of square miles, much of the land is sterilized and waterproofed, the original animals have long gone, as have primeval plants, rivers are foul, the atmosphere is polluted, climate and microclimate have retrogressed to increased violence, a million acres of land are transformed annually from farm land to hot-dog stand, diner, gas station, rancher and split level, asphalt and concrete, billboards and sagging wire, parking lots and car cemeteries; yet slums accrue faster than new buildings, which seek to replace them. The epidemiologist can speak of urban epidemics—heart and arterial disease, renal disease, cancer, and, not least, neuroses and psychoses. A serious proposition has been advanced to the effect that the modern city would be in serious jeopardy without the safeguards of modern medicine and social legislation. Lewis Mumford can describe cities as dysgenic. There has arisen the recent specter, described as "pathological togetherness," under which density and social pressure are being linked to the distribution of disease and limitations upon reproduction. We record stress from sensory overload and the response of negative hallucination to urban anarchy. When one considers that New York may well add 1,500 square miles of new "low-grade tissue" to its perimeter in the next twenty years, then one recalls Loren Eiseley's image and sees the cities of man as gray, black, and brown blemishes upon the green earth with dynamic tentacles extending from them and asks: "Are these the evidence of man, the planetary disease?"

WESTERN VIEWS: MAN AND NATURE

Yet how can nature be justified in the city? Does one invoke dappled sunlight filtered through trees of ecosystems, the shad run or water treatment, the garden in the city or negative entropy? Although at first glance an unthinkable necessity, the task of justifying nature in the city of man is, with prevailing values and process, both necessary and difficult. The realities of cities now and the plans for their renewal and extension offer incontrovertible evidence of the absence of nature present and future. Should Philadelphia realize the Comprehensive Plan, then $20 billion and twenty years later there will be less open space than there is today. Cities are artifacts becoming ever more artificial—as though medieval views prevailed that nature was defiled, that living systems shared original sin with man, that only the artifice was free of sin. The motto for the city of man seems to be: salvation by stone alone.

Of course, the medieval view of nature as rotten and rotting is only an aspect of the historic Western anthropocentric–anthropomorphic tradition in which nature is relegated to inconsequence. Judaism and Christianity have been long concerned with justice and compassion for the acts of man to man but have traditionally assumed nature to be a mere backdrop for the human play. Apparently, the literal interpretation of the creation in Genesis is the tacit text for Jews and Christians alike—man exclusively divine, man given dominion over all life and non-life, enjoined to subdue the earth. The cosmos is thought to be a pyramid erected to support man upon its pinnacle, reality exists only because man can perceive it; indeed, God is made in the image of man. From origins in Judaism, extension into classicism, reinforcement in Christianity, inflation in the Renaissance, and absorption into nineteenth- and twentieth-century thought, the anthropocentric–anthropomorphic view has become the tacit Western posture of man versus nature. The nineteenth- and twentieth-century city is the most complete expression of this view. Within the Western tradition exists a contrary view of man and nature which has a close correspondence to the Oriental attitude of an aspiration to harmony of man in nature, a sense of a unitary and encompassing natural order within which man exists. Among others, the naturalist tradition in the West includes Duns Scotus, Joannes Scotus Erigena, Francis of Assisi, Wordsworth, Goethe, Thoreau, Gerard Manley Hopkins, and the nineteenth- and twentieth-century naturalists. Their insistence upon nature being at least the sensible order within which man exists or a Manifestation of God demanding deference and reverence is persuasive to many but not to the city builders.

Are the statements of scientists likely to be more persuasive?

David R. Goddard (1960–1961): "No organism lives without an environment. As all organisms are depletive, no organism can survive in an environment of its exclusive creation."

F. R. Fosberg (1958): "An ecosystem is a functioning, interacting system composed of one or more organisms and their effective environment, both physical and biological. All ecosystems are open systems. Ecosystems may be stable or unstable. The stable system is in a steady state. The entropy in an unstable system is more likely to increase than decrease. There is a tendency towards diversity in natural ecosystems. There is a tendency towards uniformity in artificial ecosystems or those strongly influenced by man."

Paul Sears (1956): "Any species survives by virtue of its niche, the opportunity afforded it by environment. But in occupying this niche, it also assumes a role in relation to its surroundings. For further survival it is necessary that its role at least be not a disruptive one. Thus, one generally finds in nature that each component of a highly organized community serves a constructive or at any rate, a stabilizing role. The habitat furnishes the niche, and if any species breaks up the habitat, the niche goes with it . . . To persist organic systems must be able to utilize radiant energy not merely to perform work, but to maintain the working system in reasonably good order. This requires the presence of organisms adjusted to the habitat and to each other so organized to make the fullest use of the influent radiation and to conserve for use and reuse the materials which the system requires."

Complex creatures consist of billions of cells, each of which, like any single-celled creature, is unique, experiences life, metabolism, reproduction, and death. The complex animal exists through the operation of symbiotic relationships between cells as tissues and organs integrated as a single organism. Hans Selye (1961) describes this symbiosis as intercellular altruism, the situation under which the cell concedes some part of its autonomy towards the operation of the organism and the organism responds to cellular processes.

Aldo Leopold (1949) has been concerned with the ethical content of symbiosis: "Ethics so far studied by philosophers are actually a process in ecological as well as philosophical terms. They are also a process in ecological evolution. An ethic, ecologically, is a limitation on freedom of action in the struggle for existence. An ethic, philosophically, is a differentiation of social from anti-social conduct. These are two definitions of one thing which has its origin in the tendency of interdependent individuals and groups to evolve modes of cooperation. The ecologist calls these symbioses. There is as yet no ethic dealing with man's relation to the environment and the animals and plants which grow upon it. The extension of ethics to include man's relation to environment is, if I read the evidence correctly, an evolutionary possibility and an ecological necessity. All ethics so far evolved rest upon a single premise that the individual is a member of a community of interdependent parts. His instincts prompt him to compete for his place in the community, but his ethics prompt him to cooperate, perhaps in order that there may be a place to compete for."

The most important inference from this body of information is that interdependence, not independence, characterizes natural systems. Thus, man–nature interdependence presumably holds as true for urban man as for his rural contemporaries. We await the discovery of an appropriate physical and symbolic form for the urban man–nature relationship.

NATURAL AND ARTIFICIAL ENVIRONMENTS

From the foregoing statements by natural scientists, we can examine certain extreme positions. First, there can be no conception of a completely "natural" environment. Wild nature, save a few exceptions, is not a satisfactory physical environment. Yet the certainty that man must adapt nature and himself does not diminish his dependence upon natural, non-human processes. These two observations set limits upon conceptions of man and nature. Man must adapt through both biological and cultural innovation, but these adaptations occur within a context of natural, non-human processes. It is not inevitable that adapting nature to support human congregations must of necessity diminish the quality of the physical environment. Indeed, all of pre-industrial urbanism was based upon the opposite premise, that only in the city could the best conjunction of social and physical environment be achieved. This major exercise of power to adapt nature for human ends, the city, need not be a diminution of physiological, psychological, and esthetic experience.

Although there can be no completely natural environments inhabited by man, completely artificial environments are equally unlikely. Man in common with all organisms is a persistent configuration of matter through which the environment ebbs and flows continuously. Mechanically, he exchanges his substance at a very rapid rate while, additionally, his conceptions of reality are dependent upon the attribution of meaning to myriads of environmental stimuli which impinge upon him continuously. The materials of his being are natural, as are many of the stimuli which he perceives; his utilization of the materials and of many stimuli is involuntary. Man makes artifices, but galactic and solar energy, gases of hydrosphere and atmosphere, the substance of the lithosphere, and all organic systems remain elusive of human artificers.

Yet the necessity to adapt natural environments to sustain life is common to many organisms other than man. Creation of a physical environment by organisms as individuals and as communities is not exclusively a human skill. The chambered nautilus, the beehive, the coral formation, to select but a few examples, are all efforts by organisms to take inert materials and dispose them to create a physical environment. In these examples, the environments created are complementary to the organisms. They are constructed with great economy of means; they are expressive; they have, in human eyes, great beauty; and they have survived periods of evolutionary time vastly longer than the human span.

Simple organisms utilize inert materials to create physical environments which sustain life. Man also confronts this necessity. Man, too, is natural in that he responds to the same laws as do all physical and biological systems. He is a plant parasite, dependent upon the plant kingdom and its associated micro-organisms, insects, birds, and animals for all atmospheric oxygen, all food, all fossil fuel, natural fibers and cellulose, for the stability of the water cycle, and the amelioration of climate and microclimate. His dependence upon the plant and photosynthesis establishes his dependence upon the micro-organisms of the soil, particularly the decomposers which are necessary to the recycling of essential nutrients, the insects, birds, and animals which are in turn linked to survival of plant systems. He is equally dependent upon the natural process of water purification by micro-organisms. The operation of these non-human physical and biological processes is essential for human survival.

Having concluded that there can be neither a completely artificial nor a completely natural environment, we direct our attention to some determinants of optimal proportions. Some indication may be inferred from man's evolutionary history. His physiology and some significant part of his psychology derive from the billions of years of his biological history. During the most recent human phase of a million or so years, he has been preponderantly food gatherer, hunter, and, only recently, farmer. His urban experience is very recent indeed. Thus, the overwhelming proportion of his biological history has involved experience in vastly more natural environments than he now experiences. It is to these that he is physiologically adapted. According to F. R. Fosberg (1958):

It is entirely possible that man will not survive the changed environment that he is creating, either because of failure of resources, war over their dwindling supply, or failure of his nervous system to evolve as rapidly as the change in environment will require. Or he may only survive in small numbers, suffering the drastic reduction that is periodically the lot of pioneer species, or he may change beyond our recognition. . . . Management and utilization of the environment on a true sustaining yield basis must be achieved. And all this must be accomplished without altering the environment beyond the capacity of the human organism, as we know it, to live in it.

HUMAN ECOSYSTEMS

There are several examples where ecosystems, dominated by man, have endured for long periods of time, the example of traditional Japanese agriculture being perhaps the most spectacular. Here an agriculture of unequaled intensity and productivity has been sustained for over a thousand years, the land is not impoverished but enriched by human intervention, the ecosystem, wild lands, and farm lands are complex, stable, highly productive, and beautiful. The pervasive effect of this harmony of man-nature is reflected in a language remarkable in its descriptive power of nature, a poetry succinct yet capable of the finest shades of meaning, a superb painting tradition in which nature is the icon, an architecture and town building of astonishing skill and beauty, and, not least, an unparalleled garden art in which nature and the garden are the final metaphysical symbol.

In the Western tradition, farming in Denmark and England has sustained high productivity for two or more centuries, appears stable, and is very beautiful; in the United States, comparable examples exist in Amish, Mennonite, and Pennsylvania Dutch farming.

Understanding of the relationship of man to nature is more pervasive and operative among farmers than any other laymen. The farmer perceives the source of his food in his crops of cereal, vegetables, roots, beef, fish, or game. He understands that, given a soil fertility, his crop is directly related to inputs of organic material, fertilizer, water, and sunlight. If he grows cotton or flax or tends sheep, he is likely to know the source of the fibers of his clothes. He recognizes timber, peat, and hydroelectric power as

sources of fuel; he may well know of the organic source of coal
and petroleum. Experience has taught him to ensure a functional
separation between septic tank and well, to recognize the process
of erosion, runoff, flood, and drought, the differences of altitude
and orientation. As a consequence of this acuity, the farmer has
developed a formal expression which reflects an understanding
of the major natural processes. Characteristically, high ground
and steep slopes are given over to forest and woodland as a
source of timber, as a habitat for game, as an element in erosion
control, and as a water supply. The more gently sloping meadows
below are planted to orchards, above the spring frost line, or in
pasture. Here a seep, spring, or well is often the source of water
supply. In the valley bottom, where floods have deposited rich
alluvium over time, is the area of intensive cultivation. The farm
buildings are related to conditions of climate and microclimate,
above the floodplain, sheltered and shaded by the farm woodland. The septic tank is located in soils suitable for this purpose
and below the elevation of the water source.

Here, at the level of the farm, can be observed the operation of
certain simple, empirical rules and a formal expression which
derives from them. The land is rich, and we find it beautiful.

Clearly, a comparable set of simple rules is urgently required
for the city and the metropolis. The city dweller is commonly
unaware of these natural processes, ignorant of his dependence
upon them. Yet the problem of the place of nature in the city is
more difficult than that of the farmer. Nature, as modified in
farming, is intrinsic to the place. The plant community is relatively immobile, sunlight falls upon the site as does water, nutrients are cycled through the system in place. Animals in ecosystems have circumscribed territories, and the conjunction of
plants and animals involves a utilization and cycling of energy
and materials in quite limited areas. The modern city is, in this
respect, profoundly different in that major natural processes
which sustain the city, provide food, raw materials for industry,
commerce, and construction, resources of water, and pure air
are drawn not from the city or even its metropolitan area but

from a national and even international hinterland. The major natural processes are not intrinsic to the locus of the city and cannot be.

NATURE IN THE METROPOLIS

In the process of examining the place of nature in the city of man, it might be fruitful to consider initially the role of nature in the metropolitan area, as here, in the more rural fringes, can still be found analogies to the empiricism of the farmer. Here the operative principle might be that natural processes which perform work or offer protection in their natural form without human effort should have a presumption in their favor. Planning should recognize the values of these processes in decision-making for prospective land uses.

A more complete understanding of natural processes and their interactions must await the development of an ecological model of the metropolis. Such a model would identify the regional inventory of material in atmosphere, hydrosphere, lithosphere, and biosphere, identify inputs and outputs, and both describe and quantify the cycling and recycling of materials in the system. Such a model would facilitate recognition of the vital natural processes and their interdependence which is denied today. Lacking such a model, we find it necessary to proceed with available knowledge. On a simpler basis, we can say that the major inputs in biological systems are sunlight, oxygen–carbon dioxide, food (including nutrients), and water. The first three are not limiting in the metropolis; water may well be limiting both as to quantity and quality. In addition, there are many other reasons for isolating and examining water in process. Water is the single most specific determinant of a large number of physical processes and is indispensable to all biological processes. Water, as the agent of erosion and sedimentation, is causal to geological evolution, the realities of physiography. Mountains, hills, valleys, and plains experience a variety of climate and microclimate consequent upon their physiography; the twin combination of physiography and climate determines the incidence and distribution of plants and animals, their niches, and habitats. Thus, using water as the point of departure, we can recognize its impact on the making of mountains and lakes, ridges and plains, forests and deserts, rivers, streams and marshes, the distribution of plants and animals. Lacking an ecological model, we may well select water as the best indicator of natural process. In any watershed, the uplands represent the majority of the watershed area. Assuming equal distribution of precipitation and uniform ground conditions over the watershed, we know that the maximum area will produce the maximum runoff. The profile of watersheds tends to produce the steeper slopes in the uplands with the slope diminishing toward the outlet. The steeper the slope, the greater is the water velocity. This combination of maximum runoff links maximum volume to maximum velocity—the two primary conditions of flood and drought. These two factors in turn exacerbate erosion, with the consequence of depositing silt in stream beds, raising floodplains, and increasing intensity and incidence of floods in piedmont and estuary.

The natural restraints to flooding and drought are mainly the presence and distribution of vegetation, particularly on the uplands and their steep slopes. Vegetation absorbs and utilizes considerable quantities of water; the surface roots, trunks of trees, stems of shrubs and plants, the litter of the forest floor mechanically retard the movement of water, facilitating percolation, increasing evaporation opportunity. A certain amount of water is removed temporarily from the system by absorption into plants, and mechanical retardation facilitates percolation, reduces velocity, and thus diminishes erosion. In fact, vegetation stands and their soils act as a sponge restraining extreme runoff, releasing water slowly over longer periods, diminishing erosion and sedimentation, in short, diminishing the frequency and intensity of oscillation between flood and drought.

Below the uplands of the watershed are characteristically the more shallow slopes and broad plains of the piedmont. Here is the land most often developed for agriculture. These lands, too, tend to be favored locations for villages, towns, and cities. Here, forests are residues or the products of regeneration on abandoned farms. Steep slopes in the piedmont are associated with streams and rivers. The agricultural piedmont does not control its own defenses. It is defended from flood and drought by the vegetation of the uplands. The vegetation cover and conservation practices in the agricultural piedmont can either exacerbate or diminish flood and drought potential; the piedmont is particularly vulnerable to both.

The incidence of flood and drought is not alone consequent upon the upland sponge but also upon estuarine marshes, particularly where these are tidal. Here at the mouth of the watershed, at the confluence of important rivers or of river and sea, the flood component of confluent streams or the tidal component of floods assumes great importance. In the Philadelphia metropolitan area, the ocean and the estuary are of prime importance as factors in flood. A condition of intense precipitation over the region combined with high tides, full estuary, and strong onshore winds combines the elements of potential flood. The relation of environmental factors of the upland component and the agricultural piedmont to flood and drought has been discussed. The estuarine marshes and their vegetation constitute the major defense against the tidal components of floods. These areas act as enormous storage reservoirs absorbing mile-feet of potentially destructive waters, reducing flood potential.

This gross description of water-related processes offers determinism for the place of nature in the metropolis. From this description can be isolated several discrete and critical phases in the process. Surface water as rivers, streams, creeks, lakes, reservoirs, and ponds would be primary; the particular form of surface water in marshes would be another phase; the floodplain as the area temporarily occupied by water would be yet another. Two critical aspects of ground water, the aquifer and its recharge areas, could be identified. Agricultural land has been seen to be a product of alluvial deposition, whereas steep slopes and forests play important roles in the process of runoff. If we could identify the proscriptions and permissiveness of these parameters to other land use, we would have an effective device for discriminating the relative importance of different roles of metropolitan lands. Moreover, if the major divisions of upland, piedmont, and estuary and the processes enumerated could be afforded planning recognition and legislative protection, the metropolitan area would derive its form from a recognition of natural process. The place of nature in the metropolis would be reflected in the distribution of water and floodplain, marshes, ridges, forests, and farm land, a matrix of natural lands performing work or offering protection and recreational opportunity distributed throughout the metropolis.

This conception is still too bald; it should be elaborated to include areas of important scenic value, recreational potential, areas of ecological, botanical, geological, or historic interest. Yet, clearly, the conception, analogous to the empiricism of the farmer, offers opportunity for determining the place of nature in the metropolis.

NATURE IN THE CITY

The conception advocated for the metropolitan area has considerable relevance to the problem of the place of nature in the city of man. Indeed, in several cities, the fairest image of nature exists in these rare occasions where river, floodplain, steep slopes, and woodlands have been retained in their natural condition— the Hudson and Palisades in New York, the Schuylkill and Wissahickon in Philadelphia, the Charles in Boston and Cambridge. If rivers, floodplains, marshes, steep slopes, and woodlands in the city were accorded protection to remain in their natural condition or were retrieved and returned to such a condition where possible, this single device, as an aspect of water quality, quantity, flood and drought control, would ensure for many cities an immeasurable improvement in the aspect of nature in the city, in addition to the specific benefits of a planned watershed. No other device has such an ameliorative power.

Quite obviously, in addition to benefits of flood control and water supply, the benefits of amenity and recreational opportunity would be considerable. As evidence of this, the city of Philadelphia has a twenty-two mile waterfront on the Delaware. The most grandiose requirements for port facilities and water-related industries require only eight miles of waterfront. This entire waterfront lies in a floodplain. Levees and other flood-protection devices have been dismissed as exorbitant. Should this land be transformed into park, it would represent an amelioration in Philadelphia of incomparable scale.

Should this conception of planning for water and water-related parameters be effectuated, it would provide the major framework for the role of nature in the city of man. The smaller elements of the face of nature are more difficult to justify. The garden and park, unlike house, shop, or factory, have little "functional" content. They are, indeed, more metaphysical symbol than utilitarian function. As such, they are not amenable to quantification or the attribution of value. Yet it is frequently the aggregation of these gardens and spaces which determines the humanity of a city. Values they do have. This is apparent in the flight to the suburbs for more natural environments—a self-defeating process of which the motives are clear. Equally, the selection of salubrious housing location in cities is closely linked to major open spaces, which reflects the same impulse. The image of nature at this level is most important, the cell of the home, the street, and neighborhood. In the city slum, nature exists in the backyard ailanthus and sumac, in lice, cockroach, rat, cat, and mouse; in luxury highrise, there are poodles and tropical fish, and potted trees over parking garages. In the first instance, nature reflects "disturbance" to the ecologist; it is somewhat analogous to the scab on a wound, the first step of regeneration towards equilibrium, a sere arrested at the most primitive level. In the luxury highrise, nature is a canary in a cage, surrogate, an artifice, forbidden even the prospect of an arrested sere.

Three considerations seem operative at this level of concern.

The first is that the response which nature induces, tranquillity, calm, introspection, openness to order, meaning and purpose, the place of values in the world of facts, is similar to the evocation from works of art. Yet nature is, or was, abundant; art and genius are rare.

The second consideration of some importance is that nature in the city is very tender. Woodlands, plants, and animals are very vulnerable to human erosion. Only expansive dimensions will support self-perpetuating and self-cleansing nature. There is a profound change between such a natural scene and a created and maintained landscape.

The final point is related to the preceding. If the dimensions are appropriate, a landscape will perpetuate itself. Yet, where a site has been sterilized, built upon, buildings demolished, the problem of creating a landscape, quite apart from creating a self-perpetuating one, is very considerable and the costs are high. The problems of sustaining a landscape, once made, are also considerable; the pressure of human erosion on open space in urban housing and the inevitable vandalism ensure that only a small contingent of primitive and hardy plants can survive. These factors, with abnormal conditions of ground water, soil air, atmospheric pollution, stripping, and girdling, limit nature to a very constricted image.

THE FUTURE

Perhaps, in the future, analysis of those factors which contribute to stress disease will induce inquiry into the values of privacy, shade, silence, the positive stimulus of natural materials, and the presence of comprehensible order, indeed natural beauty. When young babies lack fondling and mother love, they sometimes succumb to moronity and death. The dramatic reversal of this pattern has followed simple maternal solicitude. Is the absence of nature—its trees, water, rocks, and herbs, sun, moon, stars, and changing seasons—a similar type of deprivation? The solicitude of nature, its essence if not its image, may be seen to be vital.

Some day, in the future, we may be able to quantify plant photosynthesis in the city and the oxygen in the atmosphere, the insulation by plants of lead from automobile exhausts, the role of diatoms in water purification, the amelioration of climate and microclimate by city trees and parks, the insurance of negative ionization by fountains, the reservoirs of air which, free of combustion, are necessary to relieve inversion pollution, the nature-space which a biological inheritance still requires, the stages in land regeneration and the plant and animal indicators of such regeneration, indeed, perhaps, even the plant and animal indicators of a healthy environment. We will then be able to quantify the necessities of a minimum environment to support physiological man. Perhaps we may also learn what forms of nature are necessary to satisfy the psychological memory of a biological ancestry.

Today, that place where man and nature are in closest harmony in the city is the cemetery. Can we hope for a city of man, an ecosystem in dynamic equilibrium, stable and complex? Can we hope for a city of man, an ecosystem with man dominant, reflecting natural processes, human and non-human, in which artifice and nature conjoin as art and nature, in a natural urban environment speaking to man as a natural being and nature as the environment of man? When we find the place of nature in the city of man, we may return to that enduring and ancient inquiry —the place of man in nature.

REFERENCES

Fosberg, F. R. 1958. The preservation of man's environment. *Proc. 9th Pac. Sci. Congr.* (1957) 20:160.

Goddard, David. 1960–1961. Transcript from a program in "The House We Live In" series, produced on WCAU-TV, Channel 10, Philadelphia, a thirteen-week series.

Leopold, Aldo. 1949. *A sand county almanac.* New York, Oxford University Press, pp. 202–203.

Mumford, Lewis. 1956. Prospect. In *Man's role in changing the face of the earth,* ed. by W. L. Thomas, Jr., et al., Chicago, University of Chicago Press, p. 1142.

Sears, Paul B. 1956. The processes of environmental change by man. In *Man's role in changing the face of the earth*, ed. by W. L. Thomas, Jr., et al., Chicago, University of Chicago Press, pp. 471–484.

Selye, Hans. 1961. Transcript from a program in "The House We Live In" series, produced on WCAU-TV, Channel 10, Philadelphia (January 15, 1961), a thirteen-week series.

CHALLENGE FOR SURVIVAL *Commentary*
by Bernard L. Orell

In commenting on Dr. McHarg's approach, and the title of his subject, "The place of nature in the city of man," I will devote my brief, and necessarily general, remarks to the problems with which we are faced in the city of man, their relevance to people, what motivates these people, and how they function.

The problems related to environmental quality that we face today are actually related to people, and when we refer to "people" we should speak in terms of their needs, their activities, and their desires, and how these relate to the situation in which people find themselves. Environmental quality has declined, and the trend must be turned in the other direction.

With regard to the influence of people on these trends, perhaps just a few statistics are worthwhile. It took from the beginning of man to 1850 for the first billion people to populate the earth; between 1850 and 1925, 75 years, the second billion came along; from 1925 to 1962, 37 years, the third billion arrived on the scene; it will take from 1962 to 1975, 13 years, for the fourth billion to populate the earth; and from 1975 to 1982, 7 years, for the fifth billion. This means very simply that to feed, clothe, house, educate, and entertain this rapidly increasing population, we must use wisely the resources of the country and manage intensively the environment.

In my opinion, the dignity of man grows with pride in his own self-sufficiency; it shrivels as he becomes more dependent on his neighbor. Basically, and perhaps this statement is a little at odds with Dr. McHarg's, I feel very strongly that people essentially are good. They respond to the positive, they desire the best for family, friend, associate, and the environment; but they have certain tendencies that destroy some of their abilities to relate to the environment.

First, they tend to congregate, and so we have cities. Perhaps the best illustration of this tendency is in our western country.

When the visitor arrives at Yosemite, the Grand Tetons, and the other national parks, he finds the wide open spaces he seeks, and he also finds very few developed areas. His natural gregarity makes this situation fine with him. The tents are invariably pitched close together, so close that I'm sure a private conversation cannot be carried on in one without being heard in the next. In fact, tent lines usually overlap.

People also need economic security. They need the opportunity to improve their economic well-being, and, as this is accomplished, they also need improved environmental quality that provides opportunity to reflect and determine direction, as well as cultural opportunity to complete the whole balanced person.

Finally, and perhaps most critically, the physiological fact of life is that the very act of living creates waste. The process of manufacturing the tools and providing the services that people must have also involves the creation of waste. If, therefore, proper control of the environment is to be accomplished, one of the first steps is to recognize the reality of waste and the need to control the utilization of resources and the disposal of the results of that utilization.

People, then, and their needs, constitute the basic problem with regard to environmental quality in these days of a burgeoning population. In developing an approach to the problems created by these elements, it seems to me that we should be concerned not with attempting to find a scapegoat but rather with gearing our social, economic, and industrial processes toward positive solutions leading to the improvement we must have.

Only a few years ago it was generally accepted practice to use bodies of water and air for the disposal of waste. This was not the result of a deliberate attempt on the part of a few to befoul these precious natural assets but simply to use their waste-receiving qualities which were sufficient at lower population levels. In brief, accusations towards segments of industry, municipalities, or any other specific elements of our society tend to create defensive activity, whereas a positive approach to these same factors would lead to definitive determination of problems and development of the concerted action necessary for accomplishment.

It would certainly be my hope that the company I represent and the forest-products industry as a whole could work positively for such accomplishment with the interested groups that you in this audience represent.

Specifically, with relation to the approach of the forest-products industry to environmental quality, we must of necessity clear-cut certain species of trees which have grown in even-age stands. In the past, because the public itself was not particularly concerned, we were not especially concerned with the environmental aspects of clearcutting, which certainly does leave the land looking poor until the new crop of trees begins to take over. We who are involved in the forest-products industry are also a part of the population explosion about which we have just been talking, and we, along with others, are now very concerned about environmental quality in all of its aspects. Today it is our recognized responsibility when we do clear-cut to think in terms of the esthetic as well as the silvicultural. This means added care in logging along roadsides, the leaving of understory trees, and immediate planting and seeding to return the land even more quickly to a green, growing, and beautiful condition. Dr. McHarg suggests the intensive agricultural development in Japan as an example of wise use. Forest management can and will accomplish the same esthetic effect through "wise and intensive use."

How, then, does all this relate itself to the city and the place of nature in the city? The reflection I would like to leave with you as a commentary to Dr. McHarg's approach is that, essentially, people must be influenced through education: (*a*) to not congregate, (*b*) to take care of waste individually and collectively, and (*c*) to think in terms of the natural and their need for the natural. The factors of esthetics and environment should go into all urban and suburban development.

For instance, there are service stations, industrial developments, housing projects, and even electric utility substations that blend with the natural and enhance rather than destroy environmental quality. Parking areas can have trees and gardens, and all can have natural scapes as illustrated so beautifully by our host, The Rockefeller University.

Perhaps one of the outstanding examples of accomplishment in this regard has been that of Lady Bird Johnson in beautifying even the smallest of squares, triangles, and minute open spaces in the downtown and residential area of Washington, D.C.

My commentary really then relates to the necessity for a thoughtful educational effort to have people, whether they be industrial executives, members of the intellectual community, or laborers, think in terms of the environment in which they live and of the needs that relate to that environment.

The green areas of Megalopolis JEAN GOTTMANN

The rise of Megalopolitan urban regions around the world is directly related, as we have tried to show in the second half of our study of *Megalopolis* on this northeastern seaboard, to the general evolution of modern society in the well-developed countries. This vast urban growth aims at a post-Industrial Revolution social structure, in which the majority of the labor force is occupied in non-production activities; it provides a way of life in which people enjoy greater mobility and longer periods away from their employment duties (which may be called "leisure time" or "recreational time"). Still, the Megalopolitan way of life imposes a great many rules, regulations, and disciplines on the individual, who lives in conditions of dense occupancy of the urban territory. Rapidly increasing percentages of the total population in the countries of advanced economy, that is, of the more affluent countries, spend most of their time at densities of several thousands per square mile in the residential areas, and of a hundred thousand and more per square mile in the areas where they work. Such densities of land use obviously require man-made environment in which people are divorced from the natural framework of trees, woods, fields, and so forth.

For many centuries, as cities grew large and dense, the more affluent members of the urban community surrounded their castles and mansions with parks or gardens offering a miniaturization of the so-called "natural" environment as they knew it in the rural areas surrounding the city. Private parks around castles in rural territory were usually, in days of yore, reserved for the exclusive use and enjoyment of the people in the castle. But we know that in the large cities the gardens around royal or noble mansions in the Europe of the seventeenth or eighteenth centuries were opened to the ordinary folk living in the neighborhood for their walks and enjoyment of the green space, except for the days when special functions were taking place in the gardens. By the middle of the nineteenth century, the major cities had grown too big, reaching the million size, for these arrangements still to satisfy the urban masses. A new system of public parks on a large scale was needed and, in the better managed cities, provided; the City of New York, beginning with Central Park, has often been cited as a model of that evolution, and rightly so. As the mobility, affluence, and time for recreation of the urban masses increased in the twentieth century, more green spaces became necessary to provide for the variety of recreational activities of the urban dweller. A few cities could still satisfy these needs in the immediate vicinity of residential areas (thus, Jones Beach), but in most instances it became indispensable to plan green spaces, at a distance from the city, which could be used for the outdoor recreational needs of millions of urbanites.

Suburbanization of residences and of some of the economic activities appeared temporarily as a solution, reducing the density of occupancy, at least for the homes. But as more people crowded into suburban areas, the density thickened there too. The lawns and gardens around the dwellings of many millions of the suburbanites became miniaturized themselves. To some extent, a happy balance or a symbiosis between urban and rural was achieved in some parts of this northeastern *Megalopolis,* as we described it some ten years ago. This solution, however, loses its quality and turns into a source of landscape pollution, as well as other forms of pollution; and the rising costs of services and environmental control increase as the numbers, and therefore the density, of suburban establishments rise. We are thus faced with the necessity of providing public green areas of different sizes for people in the cities and in the suburbs. This cannot be left anymore, in the large, thickening metropolitan system, to private initiative and ownership. We can see where unplanned scattering of private residences leads in the rapidly growing modern city if we look at the degree of miniaturization of nature achieved in Japan. It obviously becomes a very abstract and symbolic kind of nature. The Western city is beginning to become conscious of the need to multiply green areas of differing scales within the city, from the vest-pocket parks, which remind us of the public squares of medieval or renaissance design, to the large diversified green space of the type of Central Park, Prospect Park, or the Forêt de Soignes in Brussels.

Beyond the limits of the urbanized districts proper, our century has been providing outdoor recreation over vast open rural spaces, often used for several purposes at the same time. The agricultural or forested areas, within striking distance of the large cities for the motorized urbanite, have supplied walking, bird-watching, hunting, and fishing grounds. This again was long left to the private initiative of, and special arrangement between, urban and rural people. With increasing mass and density, and longer periods for outings, the intervention of public authorities has grown multiple and "normal." Public authorities not only protect but also raise fish and game for the fishing and hunting enjoyment of the population. State and public parks are scattered and proliferate all over the land in America, Europe, and other parts of the world. Such organization by public authorities of a park system for the enjoyment of the masses was an obvious consequence of urban growth and crowding. Now the range of nomadism of the urban dweller lengthens. The largest national parks in the United States are invaded during the better season by crowds of visitors so large as to cause congestion and to make the National Park Service plan for some new kind of rapid public transit through the parks attracting the largest crowds. It is significant that we first consider restricting the use of the individual motor car in such places as the national park, to protect the natural environment, but we still cannot resolve among ourselves to protect the urban man-made environment from the same disturbing factors of congestion and pollution. The closing of some of the roads to motor traffic in Central Park on Sundays has been an interesting first step in the needed direction.

Still, parks—national, state, and otherwise—are not and could not be large enough to accommodate all the need for green space for the consumption of affluent Megalopolitan populations. I have suggested calling "Megalopolitan" an urban region grouping in dense formation some 30 million people or more. For such large numbers, parks and other selected spots would still mean crowding at high density, especially during the days when the majority of the people would want to enjoy a green pasture. Therefore, it is already indispensable to "think big" in this domain and to plan for the use of much wider spaces than those reserved for parks and exclusive recreational use.

There remain in this country and in other parts of the world immense non-urbanized spaces. They are, of course, used for agricultural production, animal husbandry, forestry, and the like. The people permanently resident in those areas are being gradually thinned out by the process of urbanization, which concentrates people on small selected fractions of the total land area. A new complementarity must be ironed out between urban residents and a multi-purpose use of the rural areas, managed in a way that does not interfere with the production functions of these areas. This can even be made profitable to both the rural residents and the community as a whole, for the urban people would obviously be willing to contribute in one or several ways to the costs of maintenance of a better controlled environment in the wide-open rural spaces through which they would be allowed to roam for their enjoyment. Thus distant and forgotten regions could be brought into profitable use and perhaps even into the limelight.

Sedentary living used to be considered typical of the urban way of life. It may not be so any longer. Urbanites are moving around increasingly and over increasing distances. This must be taken into account when talking of the green areas of Megalopolis. These already exist at several scales or, shall we say, on different geographical levels: the urban parks of various sizes; the suburban recreational areas; the interurban farming and forest areas; and the open spaces farther on. There is a great future still in the recreational and natural value of the broad open spaces of Iowa and the Dakotas, where townsfolk may come and watch the grain rise, of Alaska, the Yukon, and even southern Utah, where the contact with nature can be provided at lower densities than at Miami Beach, the Bahamas, or Yosemite Valley.

To provide for such an organization of our still abundant environment, a great deal of thought and action in the fields of planning, legal regulation, and general environmental policy will be necessary. Since the dawn of civilization higher population densities have caused new legislative regulation to be evolved and enforced, making it possible to live and work together within the narrow limits of the resources of the past. The present trends of urbanization should make us understand that we are once more in a time of great upheaval and of great opportunity for the whole of mankind if we can adapt our ideas and concepts to the needs of the time. Megalopolis requires us to think of cities as an integral part of a wider system within which the urban is not to be opposed to the rural, but interwoven in a completely new fashion. There is growing complementarity between Megalopolis and the emptying rural spaces.

CHALLENGE FOR SURVIVAL *Commentary*

by August Heckscher

I would like first to congratulate The New York Botanical Garden on having arranged this day, and Mrs. Corning and Mrs. Strauss, the co-chairmen, for having laid out so deeply and broadly the problem areas which I think engage us all. It's interesting that in a newspaper of this very day, the *New York Daily News*, which is not known ordinarily for its liberality of views or for its large capacity for looking far ahead, this sentence occurs: ". . . that in the space of a few generations profligate Americans have taken an idyllic land, laced with mighty rivers, dotted with crystal clear lakes, manteled with the purest of air, and have transformed most of this heritage into a vast malodorous garbage pail." So the topics we discuss are not only very much in the news, but also touch, I think, the very heart of our own lives and of our own civilization.

It is with some diffidence that I comment, as I have been asked to do, on Dr. Gottmann's paper. He is so eminent an urbanist, so great an authority in the field; indeed he created the very term "megalopolis," which is the focus of our discussion. But I am emboldened by the fact that when he was working at the Twentieth Century Fund some ten years ago and I was the director, it was our habit to meet at lunch or in the course of a day's work, and I would be able to discuss with him then some of the emerging concepts which made their way into the great book. So I feel that as a commentator on his work, or at least as a sympathetic listener to him, I'm not altogether a novice.

His present paper is, needless to say, very close to my own thoughts. I would simply like to stress two points insofar as they apply very definitely to the work which we are trying to do here in the City of New York. First, Dr. Gottmann maintains, I think rightly, that given the density and the intensity of life in the modern city one simply cannot leave the role of nature and the organization of green places to chance or to the private domain. It is extraordinary, when you think of it, what richness

has been handed down to us in parks and open places. We sometimes think that ours is the first generation to have had bold
plans and to be civic-minded and to be capable of spending
large sums of money on public enterprises. But then one considers suddenly the miracle that is Central Park, the men who
before the Civil War (when New York didn't stretch north of
what is now the thirties) created in an eroded, rundown piece of
land those marvelous acres and filled them with the bridges and
the roads and the little paths that wind in and out, which we see
today and which we seek to conserve. But it's not only Central
Park. It is also The New York Botanical Garden up in the
Bronx where, before the northward thrust of the city had become wholly planned, men were able to carve out that immense
greenbelt of Van Cortland Park, Bronx Park, and Pelham Bay
Park, linked by vast green leis. Some parts, of course, have since
been eroded, but the form remains.

We do have this heritage in our city and, to a surprising extent,
in most cities of the country. The question is can we preserve it
and what will we do in matching the vision of these older generations? We can preserve it. I need hardly say that there is not a
park in the City of New York, there is not a green space any-
where in the midst of the urban complexes of this day, which is
not threatened by various forces, threatened by roads particularly. It always seems that a park is the easiest place to put
through a road, the most obvious place for a clover leaf (Alley
Pond in Queens or Van Cortland in the Bronx). Parks are
threatened by people who want to use them as garbage dumps.
We saved last spring, a really notable achievement, the Split Rock
area, a beautiful natural wetland in Pelham Bay Park, which a
decade or more before had been definitely condemned to be
filled with solid waste disposal and to have its natural characteristics completely erased.

We must, as I say, match the vision of these older men. I simply
mention two areas in this city where it seems to me that creative
thinking and the most courageous action are necessary. First,
we have Staten Island, containing a magnificent ridge which

runs the length of the island, a great outcropping of rock and of nature which distinguishes the island. It has remained for thirty years under the threat of a great road to be built across it. The final decision is going to be made within the next weeks or months. There in Staten Island we have the possibility of creating an immense green space. Professor McHarg has been doing a study for us of the ecology of the island, and he has shown that virtually every test applicable from the point of view of ecology and of nature reinforces the wholeness and the beauty of that area. Secondly, we have today bits and pieces of a glorious confederation of green spaces, if you will: La Tourette Park, the Davis Wildlife Refuge, Willowbrook Park, and Barrett Park, a high rock. (There are, of course, also the works of man, such as the Richmond town restoration.) If we can save that and keep it all in one, more or less, continuous belt we will have something of which future generations can be as proud as we are, for example, of Central Park. And then at Jamaica Bay we find in the 12,000 acres which the bay itself represents one of the great bird refuges, one of those great possibilities for nature being preserved in all its mystery, the whole web of life being exemplified for this and for later times. This area lies challenged by pollution, first of all, by people who want to use the land for various purposes, by the discussions (not yet final plans) for extending the runways out at Kennedy Airport, which would obliterate so much of the natural life of this place. This is my first concern: we can, and we must, keep in the midst of our city green spaces proportionate to the needs of the modern citizen.

The second point that Dr. Gottmann stressed very strongly is that we must mesh these green spaces with the rural areas, or the outer areas, beyond the city itself. He pointed out so well, I think, that as the cities become ever denser there is a tendency for the life around the cities to grow somewhat less dense. These are interesting statistics, I believe: there are more deer in megalopolis today than there were in the times of the Indians and more horses than before the automobile was invented. Or perhaps there are more horses now than ten years ago. Be that as it may, there is another fact which Dr. Gottmann discovered and has made known to us: that there are opportunities outside the cities which we must grab quickly if we are to save and exploit them.

In our way, here in the Parks Department of New York, perhaps symbolically, if you will, we are trying to link the cities to these outer greenways. We are arranging, for example, a bicycle train which will take us and our bicycles out to the end of Long Island where a day of riding has been planned. We are bussing children, increasingly during the hot summer months, out to the state parks, again trying to link the outer and the inner green places.

Many of us here are concerned with the preservation of the Hudson River. It is, after all, the frontier that lies beyond New York, beyond the city itself. A great possibility exists of creating a corridor to the wildness of the Adirondacks through some of the most beautifully cultivated lands that man has developed in this country, as well as through some of the area's greatest natural glories. The Hudson River, insofar as it can be purified and its banks preserved, will be an inestimable addition to the values and to the beauties of New York. So, I say, within the city we need courage and we need vision, but we also need largesse of view in linking the city itself to the areas around it.

Acquiring and protecting land PAUL BROOKS

When I was invited to take part in this symposium, I wondered what useful contribution a layman could make to such a distinguished professional group. I decided to limit myself to the story of land conservation in a single suburban town during the thirty-four years that I have known it. Obviously the story is of no great importance in itself. My hope is that, as a specific case history, it may be relevant to the experience of hundreds of towns which are subject to similar pressures from a nearby metropolis, and which recognize similar responsibilities to the broader community as a whole.

The town is Lincoln, Massachusetts, fifteen miles west of Boston, on the near side of Concord. Formerly a farming community, it is now inhabited largely by commuters. Thirty years ago the population was under two thousand, today it is approximately five thousand. Its growth has been steady but not explosive. The town (which in New England is synonymous with township) comprises about fifteen square miles of rolling country, much of it still in woods and open fields. There is one large body of water, formerly known as Flint's Pond, now the town reservoir. This was a favorite haunt of Henry David Thoreau, who once remarked that the world is more to be enjoyed than used: a challenge to the prevailing concept of land as a mere commodity. Unfortunately, many of his contempo-

Reprinted from *Garden Journal* 18(6): 190–194, 1968; lightly edited.

raries considered Thoreau a worthless bum. When he asked permission to build his hut on the shores of Flint's Pond, he was refused, and he had to settle instead for some land belonging to his friend Emerson on the shores of Walden. He took his revenge, however, in his immortal polemic against the owner, whom he described as "Some skin-flint, who loved better the reflecting surface of a dollar, or a bright cent, in which he could see his own brazen face—who thought only of its money value; —who would carry the landscape, who would carry his God, to market, if he could get anything for him." There is more eloquence than logic in this diatribe. The owner may simply have been afraid that Thoreau would set the woods on fire—as he did elsewhere on one occasion. But it is true that even today we know people who recognize only the money value of land; who would carry the landscape itself to market if they could.

Let me review briefly the steps that we have taken to preserve open space, and to keep at least some of our landscape off the market. In 1929, by vote of the town meeting, the minimum size of a house lot was set at 10,000 square feet. In 1936, when the completion of the turnpike from Boston to Concord threatened the town with "bulldozer developments" by outside real estate speculators, the minimum was increased to one acre. (I well remember the town meeting that year, at which the farmers and the commuters voted as a unit.) In 1955, to slow down the postwar rush to the suburbs, the figure was increased to two acres, where it stands today. Although such measures are essential to control rampant development, they obviously do not preserve sizeable tracts of open space. And as land prices continue to rise, one is faced with the additional problem of providing opportunity for families of moderate income—or, to put it another way, of preventing Lincoln from becoming a "rich man's town." One of the best methods of providing both open space and moderate priced housing is, of course, cluster zoning, which we are now actively encouraging. We have had two professional planning studies: one in 1958, using matching funds from the urban planning assistance program, and another more thorough land use study in 1965. The latter included a detailed map showing the areas recommended for preservation as open space and setting up priorities. This has become known as the "By '70 Plan," which may indicate over-optimism on our part. In any event, it serves as the basic guideline for an ambitious land acquisition program, which would comprise upwards of one thousand acres, about 10 per cent of the town.

In our day-by-day operations (or I should better say night-by-night operations, since this is all done after office hours) we have four principal tools, two of them public, and two of them private. First is zoning, which is administered by the Planning Board. Second is land purchase by the town, administered by the Conservation Commission. Third is the Lincoln Land Conservation Trust, a private "charitable trust." Fourth is another recently formed private organization, the Rural Land Foundation. People keep asking why we need so many agencies to accomplish the same thing. The answer is, of course, that each has its own special use and that all four are necessary, often working in very close cooperation.

Our zoning by-laws set the ground rules for all development. The by-laws can be strict, if you have a board of appeals to act as a safety valve in cases of obvious hardship. Ours now include an open-space conservation zone to protect wetlands from draining, filling, and building, the restrictions being similar to those for floodplain zoning. This is not imposed by the town, but is a matter of voluntary agreement by each landowner concerned. It has been used to preserve the town's primary drainage system, encompassing a sizeable pond and the brook and the swamps above and below it. I speak from personal knowledge when I say that the implementation of such a voluntary program, involving here some twenty individual landowners, requires a good many hours of persuasion. However, most landowners come to realize that the neighborhood as a whole is upgraded by such protection, to the mutual benefit of everyone.

The second and major tool is acquisition by the town of land for open space: by outright purchase, by conservation easements, or by gifts. In 1958 an official Conservation Commission was established, as required by Massachusetts law to qualify a town for matching funds from the Department of Natural Resources. Our first appropriation for land purchase was a modest $7,000, representing at that time one dollar on the tax rate. As the assessment of the town has increased, the annual appropriation has increased with it. Currently, in accordance with the advice of our professional planners, we have stepped up the program through long-term borrowing. As land prices rapidly rise, it is now or never. Our expectation, so far fulfilled, is that the town will recover 50 per cent, and probably 75 per cent, of the purchase price through a combination of state and federal aid. In the long run, the result of the program will be to keep the tax rate down, since the same land, if subdivided for house lots, would cost the town far more in services (principally schools) than it would contribute to the tax base.

Our two private agencies play a smaller but essential part. The Land Conservation Trust was set up originally to meet a specific emergency when the shore of the town reservoir was threatened. Its purposes are identical to those of the Conservation Commission. It is also developing a system of trails and bridle paths throughout the town. By serving as an organization for receipt of tax-deductible gifts of land, it makes quick, coordinated action possible. For example, when a nine-acre tract of pasture suddenly came on the market, the five abutters were prepared to buy it to keep it open. But to divide it among themselves would have been a long and expensive process. The same object was achieved by each contributing his share of the purchase price to the Land Trust, which then took title to the pasture— on which, I am glad to say, the sheep still graze, blissfully unaware of the machinations that have assured their survival.

Of course we recognize that it is neither possible, nor even desirable, to keep all our remaining open land from being developed. The question is, what *kind* of development? This is where our newest tool, the Rural Land Foundation, comes in. The Foundation was organized by a group of private citizens to see that land which is going to be subdivided anyway is sub-divided properly. With a bank loan guaranteed by the members, the Foundation buys the land and employs its own landscape architect to make a subdivision plan, reserving a sizeable tract of open space to be held by the Land Trust. It then markets the lots, which, needless to say, are larger and—particularly because of the open land—more attractive than they would be if a real estate speculator were trying to squeeze out the last penny of profit. In its first trial, this enterprise has worked without a hitch. The guarantors have never had to worry about their commit-ment. And since this is a non-profit organization, any favorable balance constitutes a revolving fund to be applied again as need arises. It is a simple scheme, which I hope will become more widely used in other suburban areas.

These are our four principal tools. Before I leave the subject, I should like to return for a moment to that question we are so often asked—why do we need all these different agencies to accomplish the same purpose? Let me give you one concrete example. An area of some thirty acres was to be subdivided: a tract of woods and swamp with trails and bridle paths, obviously an asset to the town if kept as open space. The owner was not a real estate speculator, he simply had to sell off his backland to pay for his own house. He had enough high land for nine new house lots. This is what happened. The Town, through its conserva-tion fund, bought part of the land for a modest sum. A private abuttor bought an adjacent section and donated it to the Land Trust—to which the owner also deeded the unbuildable swamp areas. The Planning Board, with the approval of the Board of Appeals, waived its requirement for a standard subdivision road, provided that only two large lots were sold, at the edge of the property.

As the arithmetic worked out, this great saving in develop-ment costs more than made up for the income lost by selling all nine house lots. The owner was happy, and the people of the Town still have their woods and trails.

So much for the methods. Whether or not they are the best

methods is a question that we must continuously reconsider. Now for a brief comment on the principles involved.

To many sociologists, everything I have been saying stems straight from the dark ages. *Suburbia*, written by Robert C. Wood, a resident of Lincoln, states: "Lincoln is undoubtedly an anachronism and is probably obstructive to the larger purposes of the Boston region." The small town, according to this theory, mirrors the worst aspects of American life. By taking this "grass-roots" approach, to use a favorite epithet, we confuse fraternity with democracy, and stifle individualism. We create communities peopled by our own kind. We reject the benefits of megalopolis. We cling to the past, although we belong to a nation that "has always shown a commitment to the proposition that growth and change are beneficial."

Maybe so, in terms of social theory, although no one who has attended a New England town meeting can seriously complain about the lack of either democracy or individualism. In terms of land use, however, this attack on the small town misses the whole point. If growth and change were automatically beneficial, the present symposium would be superfluous. The question is: what *kind* of growth and what *kind* of change? A town with a long tradition of self-government, run by people who know and care about every field and stream and woodlot, is not to be confused with an artificially created suburb. There must be hundreds of such towns in the area that we are concerned with here. At their best, they are better custodians of the land than any metropolitan government. To ignore the value of such local and personal commitment is to omit from the balance sheet its most important fixed asset.

Nor is our open space program inconsistent with our place in the larger community. As Charles W. Eliot said in his report: "Different parts of a metropolitan region should be expected to serve different purposes, peculiar to physical conditions, history and potentialities of the particular area." I confess that I find this pattern of diversity more appealing than, for example, a scheme proposed by metropolitan planners for a "glittering mosaic of balanced communities, their orderly constellations of small towns geometrically placed around the outskirts of a metropolis." I am reminded of a seventeenth century book by Bishop Burnet entitled *Sacred theory of the earth,* in which he complains that the stars are not graded according to size and symmetrically arranged in the heavens.

Finally, we have all heard the criticism that land preservation is somehow snobbish and undemocratic, that it favors the rich and the already established. I believe that the opposite is true. The land we save is open to all. "No Trespassing" signs are supplanted by trail markers and notices beginning "You are welcome" to walk, ride, and so on, provided, in short, that you don't leave litter or set the woods on fire. (People who are willing to use their legs seldom do either.) The small landowner, or the visitor from more crowded communities, has space to move around in at no cost to himself. Hard-headed real estate men are not unaware of these values. I have long been amused by the sales slogan of a development just beyond the town limits where open space has all but disappeared. "Lots for sale: In Waltham, on the Lincoln line."

However, the criticism that we are obstructing progress serves a real purpose. It keeps us aware of our responsibilities to the greater metropolitan region. While we all recognize that "open space does not have to be in public use to serve a public purpose," its very existence constitutes an obligation to adjacent communities. The concept behind our open space program is indeed an ancient one in the Anglo-Saxon world. It is the old concept of "common land"—a phrase that might well be used more often in the literature of planning. Underlying it is the realization that land is not a commodity but a trust. True ownership of a piece of land resides not solely with the holder of the deed, but with all those who know and love it.

CHALLENGE FOR SURVIVAL *Commentary*

by Bruce Quayle

When Paul Brooks wondered what contribution he, as a layman, might make to this session, he at least had had the experience of direct participation in a land conservation project. I come without even those credentials, however, and really come less as a commentator on his paper than as a reporter on another aspect of the problem of acquiring and protecting land. This is an aspect that I have observed as one responsible for my company's conservation-based advertising program.

This program is now in its fourteenth year, and by relating conservation stories it seeks to educate people on America's rich, natural heritage and to encourage them to conserve this heritage by their own actions and by supporting groups and legislation so directed. It is a program in opposition to those who, in Thoreau's words, "would carry the landscape to market." From its beginning, the program struck a responsive chord in the American conscience, and we have been gratified by those who, through the years, have said: "Well done—spread the word." But more pertinent to this meeting is the fact that we have heard from many thousands who are looking for help and advice in the acquisition and protection of land.

These are people who seek for their communities the type of program carried on in Lincoln, Massachusetts, but who are uncertain how to proceed and are unaware of the resources available to them. We have seen, first-hand, a great need for practical how-to-do-it conservation information.

Last year we received a letter from a man in Rochester who is engaged in a project to protect a piece of land from residential development—a letter that had across the top of it in capital letters: HELP, HELP, HELP. We heard from a lady in suburban New York who said: "We are trying to protect a beautiful marsh and would be grateful for any information you can give us."

From Pennsylvania, a lady wrote: "I have found there is

nothing I can do without a name or big money. I would like to learn from anyone who has overcome this materialistic monopoly." A dentist in Illinois said: "I feel that if the area residents could be made aware of our plans, we might get some help from them." We heard from far-off places like New Zealand and the Netherlands. A man from Canada wrote about an ad we had run on how a marsh had been saved, and said: "We are stumbling about as much as you mentioned."

Clearly there is a need to spread information on how to acquire and how to protect land. Willingness and desire do exist. People are ready to take action, but they need to know how. And I think that the experience of the people in Lincoln is a case study that should aid and inspire people in communities across the country.

In an advertisement published last year, we offered a folder that gave some case histories of how private citizens had preserved certain natural areas. And in the folder we listed ten conservation organizations to which one could write for help. The man who wrote "HELP, HELP, HELP" was referred to these groups, because we are not experts—we are just reporters and advocates.

Throughout the year, we had almost 12,000 requests for this folder, and I cite this figure not in praise of our printed piece, but as a measure of the desire that people have to know of programs such as that Paul Brooks described. We know that conservation programs can be carried out by individual communities and by groups without a financial angel. And our program has shown us that word of this must be spread.

There is no dearth of information. Many organizations, such as the League of Women Voters, the Isaac Walton League, the Conservation Foundation, the Nature Conservancy, and many others I probably should be mentioning, have published materials on aspects of local conservation programs. Perhaps too much material is being prepared and not enough is being done to get it out on the firing line. And perhaps, too, there is some reluctance among a few conservation organizations to spread the word about the programs of others. We had the somewhat discouraging ex-

perience of having one such association decline to run some of our
ads in its publication, because these referred to the efforts of other
conservation groups in aiding local projects. Apparently, this
organization didn't need the money either.

One group which we have come across that certainly has no
"ax to grind" is the Citizens Advisory Committee on Recreation
and Natural Beauty, with which many of you are probably
familiar. This group has just pulled together the sort of handbook
on local action that the 12,000 people who wrote to us last year
were really looking for. It is called "Community Action for
Natural Beauty," and it is a gem.

In the preface of the handbook, Laurance Rockefeller (who is
chairman of the committee) summed up the situation that exists:
"New federal and state programs are providing technical aid and
money for local action, but there are so many of these programs
that it is difficult to know where to start, and how to fit them
together."

Had he wanted to be specific, Mr. Rockefeller could have
noted, I imagine, that many people in Massachusetts may be
unaware of the state's provisions for setting up local conservation
commissions, such as was done in Lincoln. They don't know
about matching state and federal programs for local conservation
projects.

Thus, the Citizens Advisory Committee Guide. It does not try
to be definitive: it concentrates on principal approaches to the
local situations, how each approach works, and where one can
go for help. An appendix lists the many state and private agencies
available for help and the detailed manuals that can be obtained.
These are the sort of things people want to know as they seek to
acquire and protect land.

So my reporter's commentary is simple. People want to know
how to carry on a program such as the one Paul Brooks described
today, and I hope this symposium can be a stimulus for spreading
the word. And my only other comment would be that if you
have not seen the Citizens Advisory Committee Guide, you
should get hold of one. It's a dandy.

Ecology and management of the rural and the suburban landscape FRANK E. EGLER

INTRODUCTION: THE UNITY
OF MAN-PLUS-HIS-TOTAL-ENVIRONMENT

I consider it a datum of considerable historic import that there should even be a symposium of this title, "Challenge for Survival." I would say that ten years ago, were such a title suggested, it would have been considered inflammatory, controversial, activist, and certainly not one to be linked with a respected scientific organization. We should all congratulate ourselves that we *can* talk on this topic, or at least parry with the subject.

I confess that I myself might not so entitle this symposium—but maybe that is why I never have the chance to handle such matters. I would think that a suitable title would be "Is There Intelligent Life Upon Earth?" This is a phrase by no means original, but it relates to a subject well worth candid and open discussion, one that will weave in and out of our present program. It is a question you will be repeatedly asking yourself, as it pertains to human society, to this audience, or to the speakers on this platform. After all, there is no use challenging ourselves unless we *do* have enough intelligence to meet the challenge.

To place my suggested title in a different perspective, it might be said that at the moment I am—if I may use the jargon of a current best-seller—addressing 350 naked apes. I admit you are trying to cover up the condition. Yet, judging from some of the things I have seen walking the streets of New York City, we have not advanced too far. It is true also—if I may move along the time scale—to say that we are a society of Paleolithic hunters or, better, Neolithic farmers. The geneticists are firm in stating that we have not changed essentially since those times, even though they admit that the cranial capacity of our Neanderthal forebears was greater than our own. A very interesting point for sober and serious discussion would be whether we really have changed since so-called civilization began. Presumably a species evolves by survival of the fit. Yet there are interesting interlacings of ideas as to the effects of "democracy," "equality," and "humanitarianism" on the survival of the *un*fit, even on the survival of intelligence itself, which ideas presumably we do not face at *this* symposium.

To confuse still further the issue as to the standing and understanding of man in the Total Ecosystem we might consider an interesting problem that the Ford Motor Company faced in 1967. The company was using live baboons in high-speed highway test crashes. This information escaped to the public, and created some adverse comments. To this social need, and possibly with one eye cocked on the well-being of his parish and thus on his own collection plates, a gentleman of the Archdiocese of Detroit issued a statement that I consider a paragon of ecologic illiteracy. He said: "God intended animals and all creation to contribute to the well-being of man. Any use that contributes to something as important as highway safety is in keeping with God's very reason for creating lesser beings." I would like to hear Ralph Nader discuss the subject. After all, automobile accidents *are* a problem, and utilizing dumb animals is undoubtedly a better solution than such uncivilized and costly approaches as better roads, better law enforcement, reducing the horsepower so that cars cannot go 120 miles an hour, or teaching drivers to operate their vehicles in a responsible manner. It would appear that the technologically sound approach is to force baboons to ape humans behind the wheel, so that people can go on driving like monkeys.

Clearly, concerning the intelligence of man, many questions remain. As to what you will be hearing from this platform today and tomorrow, I doubt—I am referring especially to myself—that you will be hearing anything new. These things have been said again and again and again. There is a huge literature on the subject, for those of you who can and will read. It was Stewart Udall who commented, on the flyleaf of our program: "These issues should not remain in meeting halls of those who are already convinced." All we can do from the platform is to reconvince you, and then trust you will go out among men, and preach to convince those others. The challenge lies with *you*, the audience, and whether *you* follow through with thoughtful and innovative programs, at all levels of our society, that *will* allow this civilization to survive. I have hopes, or I would not have left my "territory" in the Berkshires to come here to your violent and polluted city.

There is no question as to the accuracy of the symposium title. Bold and definitive stands are being taken by a long succession of outstanding scientists and intellectual thinkers, by scientific societies, conservation and natural resource organizations, government agencies, academe, intelligent and informed citizens, and even industry (as we should be hearing from this platform). The problem is basic to the emerging new science of Human Ecosystem Ecology. This term is by no means to be confused with the "plant ecology" or "animal ecology" that was taught thirty years ago and still is taught as a course in the biology departments of many universities. This ecology is not that of the environmental relations of separate species of organisms (the so-called Fifth Level of Integration), or of populations of organisms currently called Ethology (Sixth Level), or of plant-and-animal communities (Seventh Level), or of plant-animal-soil-climate natural ecosystems, plus whatever parameters your grant-money allows you to feed into the computer (Eighth Level). Human Ecosystem Ecology is a Ninth-Level dream that involves the unity of man-plus-his-total-environment.

The Challenge for the Survival of our Total Human Ecosystem—if we may grossly simplify the problem for the moment

—lies in two dimensions: firstly, Man himself and the increasing human populations; secondly, the Total Environment and its undesirable alterations.

The problem of ever-increasing human populations can only provide us with "mathematical models" (current Academese of the High Priests of a Latter-Day Numerology) that in turn lead to unbalanced equations—except on the part of the pathologically compulsive optimist, thinking of his own short-term profits. We hear much talk about increasing the food supply. Nonsense! We can increase it to a certain point in a finite world, but when the human population is already increasing faster than the food supply is, there are more hungry people every year. Food is part of the problem but cannot solve it alone. We hear much talk about growing economies, gross national products, higher wages, higher sales, higher profits, higher dividends, higher production, higher consumption, and higher affluence. Nonsense! In a finite world, growth cannot be infinite for the parameters which are conventionally recognized by the ecologically illiterate economists. We hear much talk about birth control under the aegis of "family planning." Nonsense! Family planning involves a little ecosystem which is the family itself; and it is in our biologic inheritance to want children. Until planning gets to be on the national and international levels, there will be no solution to the problem. Increasing food, growing economies, and family planning are not stopping the burgeoning human populations. And yet there is reason now to believe that the world's population *is already* beyond what the world can adequately support in a continuing civilization of quality. There is but one solution to the present population problem, and that is a roll-back from present levels.

The problem of undesirable alterations to the Total Environment is documented profusely. We have altered the chemical balances of that environment: we now have copper, zinc, lead, arsenic, smog, persistent nerve poisons called pesticides, less oxygen, and more carbon dioxide in the atmosphere. We have altered the physical balances: our big dam engineers are doing far more than building dams that produce lakes. Upstream river balances are altered as well as downstream flows and sedimentation and, in turn, the entire coastal balances of erosion and deposition. More noise; less space; less privacy. Exhaustion of natural resources, for which the answer is *not* "conservation." Conservation far too often is only a slowing down in the process of ultimate exhaustion of our resources, so that our grandchildren inherit the problem, and the blame. Our clever technologists have been surpassingly successful in altering the environment—altering it first, then worrying about it afterwards—so that we have already produced an environment quite different from that in which we evolved. It will be interesting to see whether we can either survive that change or evolve rapidly enough *to* survive. In either instance, every thinking ecologist today is more than troubled. He is worried. We are not like the seabirds on the islands off Peru, capable of living upon 300 feet of their own guano. *They* have a clean ocean for miles around.

Linked to these two problems of human population and total environment, and on the opposite side of the coin from the topic I was assigned (rural and suburban landscape), is the problem of urbanity itself. Man did not evolve in an urban environment. It is the small village which developed at the dawn of civilization five thousand years ago and which alone has persisted in an essentially stable fashion through those millennia. On the other hand, as moths go to flames to singe their wings, people collect in cities, there to develop the greatest victory and vice. Cities, however, have risen and fallen with the centuries, each built on the ruins directly below. Babylon, Nineveh, Athens, Rome. Babylon was build on a floodplain; destroyed by a flood, as the story of Noah reveals; and *still* we build on floodplains. I am waiting to see sound, objective, scientific studies of urbanity, of the inhumanity of urbanity. So far, we are only putting salve on symptoms. Poverty, unemployment, violence, and slums are *symptoms* of a diseased social system, and do not vanish with the false affluence of money, jobs, police, and housing. History has just documented (1968) its greatest rat hole. Forty million dollars went down it, for the delectation, I am sure, of future urban ecologists. It is not rat control that was needed, but garbage control. Besides, rat meat is a wasted natural resource. I would far sooner eat a well-prepared rat stew than a concoction a neighbor of mine used to prepare from squirrels, in which the still-eyed head would stare up at one from the bottom of the bowl. The problems of the inhumanity of urbanity must be tackled in the light of a total ecology. Money should not be thrown down rat holes, any more than a case of gin should be thrown down the gutter instead of into the alcoholic. The basic problem is not cured this way.

THE RURAL AND SUBURBAN LANDSCAPE

Within the context of the unity that is man-plus-his-total-environment, we have on the one hand those solid agglomerations of humanity called cities, which suck in clean air, clean water, and food, and disgorge polluted air, polluted water, and waste. On the other hand, surrounding the cities and in various degrees of transition with them is the greenery of the rural and suburban landscape. I was originally trained as a plant ecologist, although at various times I have tried to hide that fact, apologize for it, or abdicate from it. I assume it is in the field of this specialty, which I prefer to call Vegetation Science and Vegetation Management, that the planners of this symposium wish me to speak.

My thesis on the actual Ninth-Level Management of this landscape is that the interaction of short-term private initiative, freedom, and equality with (inadequate) long-term concepts of planning and quality, has given us a rural and suburban landscape which (except for a few rare instances) cannot be occupied by urban man without its very quality being destroyed. Linear bits of urbanity are stripjoints along our highways; billboards hide the landscape; housing developments can be the epitome of tastelessness; architecture is giving way to mere "building"; dam engineers build dams with our tax money for their own pleasure; highwaymen build highways for their own pleasure, all with an illiteracy on the subject of Total Ecology that is appalling. The rural and suburban landscape has been MISmanaged, and a million dollars or so devoted to the study of that mismanagement would be money well spent.

My thesis on the theoretical Ninth-Level Science of this landscape is that much sound scientific information on the management of the greenery does exist, but it is locked up in obscure publications and in the heads of certain ecologists, including some here today. The scientists are poor communicators to society, even though they may be effective with the captives of a classroom. Too often, the scientific practice in society is short-term, empirical, and rule-of-thumb. Ecologists themselves can compound the problem, especially when they continue to believe, for example, in certain delightful and pleasing ideas of vegetation change (which they call "plant succession"). These ideas have all the instinctual fascination of legends and myths in the history of the human race and are only to be understood in that light. I have long challenged ecologists to reveal a single sound published research paper to bear up the statements I find in textbooks on this subject. I have had no takers. And I have, for a long time, offered a price of one thousand dollars for any new research study that proves the validity of the stage-by-stage relay of invaders and drop-outs that constitute the plant-succession-to-climax dogma. I have had no takers. Shall we say merely that there is room for improvement?

Among the various types of greenery in the rural and suburban landscape, we may single out five major categories for brief discussion at this time.

The home grounds. Unquestionably the professional landscapers and horticulturists have done wonders to make the American home grounds a thing of beauty. This is the domain of lawns, lawnmowers, subsoil called topsoil, alien species that are susceptible to every known form of pest, disease, and inherent weakness. The whole is kept alive by an inordinate amount of expensive care and attention, comparable to our practices in homes for the aged and the incurable. In my opinion, the Home Landscape is largely a sick environment, kept alive by sprays, sprays, and more sprays. It is a very interesting sociological phenomenon, aided and abetted by all the short-term profit-making industries, as well as by the staffs of our agricultural experiment stations who can be remarkably illiterate when it comes to Total Ecology.

I see a friend of mine in the back row of this auditorium. He was once concerned about a bulletin, distributed by a leading college of agriculture, which recommended routine treatments with persistent pesticidal sprays, regardless of whether the plants needed them or not. Such sprays did affect the plants, but they also affected the Total Environment for miles around. He wrote to the dean of this college, and received in return a classic letter that I do hope gets published some day—that is, when the dean is dead and gone. The dean missed the point of my friend's ecologic objections; he stated that this was a very successful and popular bulletin and *therefore*, presumably, it was scientifically and technologically sound. In other words, what is popular, is "right"—like alcohol, tobacco, and drugs. Scientists are human beings, the citizen must not forget.

Our parks. We have another type of greenery in our urban and suburban areas, and that is the city park. Their problems are manifold and almost insoluble, as every Director of Parks knows all too well. They could be places of beauty, peace, contentment, and health-giving recreation, as they still are in many European cities. Instead, all too often, we find them frequented by criminals at night, by vagrants in the day. They are considered as undeveloped open space to be used as garbage dumps, for appropriation by highway departments, to be taken for museum buildings, for schools and universities, for parking lots, even for commercial restaurants.

The example of Meriden, Connecticut, is illuminating. This city is in the process of losing all three of its city parks. The State Highway Department was fought by a virile and active committee of citizens. Yet, it was the apathy of the general citizens which was responsible for losing the parks when the matter came to a city vote. New York City itself has been in the news because of a related problem, that of Columbia University's proposed new gymnasium, to be built on parkland of Morningside Heights. Even though this problem is highly complex and ramifying, it is the low value placed upon parkland that is a keynote factor.

In the last analysis, our society does not use or manage its parks for the recreational, educational, and research purposes for which they are so admirably adapted. Here is the *space* which man the naked ape so much needs. And yet he is forever whittling it away. Indeed, when men do converge upon a park (have you seen an Adirondack lakeshore campground from the air, in summer?), the very quantity of humanity and of its automobiles leaves no room for greenery itself—except in the distance. As with all these situations, it is man, not the land, that needs management.

Forest lands. Tree-covered lands anastomose and intersperse all through our rural and suburban areas in much of North America. Although wood—timber, firewood, charcoal—was once their chief product, they are now often a cultural amenity to the owner, who pays land taxes but does not harvest the trees.

Forestry in one sense is the management of forest lands for any resource of value which they possess. In the historically restricted sense, forestry is management for timber. I am not unacquainted with the field. I entered a forestry college as a student in 1929; I was a professor in one for almost a decade; for one brief but humorous episode I was Senior Dendrologist of the United States Forest Service. My opinion is that at present forestry is largely an empirical, rule-of-thumb, short-sighted technology, concerned with the present crop of timber and the establishment and development of the immediately succeeding crop. I say this despite the obeisances made to grazing, hunting, fishing, and recreation. Yet I am optimistic about the future, for when our forestry colleges adopt the broader view of a Total Ecology, and thus attract students of varied and broader views, our forest lands themselves will be understood and managed, not as an isolated little box of the Total Environment, but as an integral part of the whole.

Wildlife lands. If forest lands have their problems, wildlife lands have greater problems, largely because wildlife science is in a still more primitive stage of development than forestry. Furthermore, there is an inherent paradox that may long restrain its development. Wildlife is largely a product of its environment, and that environment is largely green vegetation. To understand wildlife, one must understand vegetation also. Yet wildlife professionals are animal-lovers, not plant-lovers. The absence of a vegetational sophistication in the wildlife literature—exceptions proving the generalization—is as pathetic as it is amusing.

Animals, from mice to moose, from bees to birds, are far more than part of the aesthetics and quality of our Total Environment for the hunter or for the watcher. They are integral components of a healthy Total Environment, from the earthworms which plow and loosen the soil to the insects which pollinate the crops, to the rodents which cache the seeds, to the large predators which hold other populations in check. In other words, animals are but one strand in the web of the Total Ecosystem. We need wildlife specialists; even more, we need wildlifers who are also Total Ecologists.

There is room for improvement. I recently took occasion to—what shall we say?—comment upon (possibly that is a mild term) the entire wildlife profession, in the form of a review of a certain publication on wildlife habitat management, revealing it as dominated by short-sighted, how-to-do-it technicians. I fully expected to hear some outraged squawks and growls. To my knowledge, only one letter was received by the Editor, and that was by the Executive Secretary of the Wildlife Society, who essentially agreed with me on all points! Shall we say that the room for upgrading the science is recognized by the people themselves—and thus I am optimistic, within limits.

Government highways and corporate rightofways. As the fifth point in this all-too-short discussion of the types of greenery in the rural and suburban landscape, we refer to a type of land which many of you may not have thought about: the sides of our highways, the transmission lines of electric utility corporations, the pipelines of our oil companies, the telephone lines with the greenery underneath. The aggregate of this land was estimated ten years ago to be over 50,000,000 acres in continental United States. That is more acreage than all six New England states have together.

The scientific know-how for managing this land, at lowest cost for the most years with the highest conservation values, has been hanging around since 1949, waiting to be utilized. And yet this enormous acreage, that can add so much to the quality of our total environment, has been for twenty years in the hands of the chemical industry, which has in turn influenced the commercial sprayers, who have in turn influenced the utility corporations and highwaymen—the whole creating a network of social units that must thoroughly delight the cynic.

To convince you how difficult it is to impart this scientific information to a society that will use it, that is, to a Total Human Ecosystem, I need recount but one tale. It was at one of the highly influential, industry-sponsored, weed control conferences in the hotel suite of one of the leading chemical manufacturers, at two o'clock in the morning—when men, especially those men, get honest. "Frank," said a sales executive, "I don't know a goddam about botany. I sort of think you're right, but you are wasting your time with us. We can't sell enough chemical your way." He was entirely correct. Properly done, with or without chemicals, this vegetation can be managed extremely cheaply. My demonstration firebreak, in Sullivan County, New York, of low stable vegetation has not had one dollar spent on it since 1932, and there are yet no unwanted invading trees. There could be tremendous savings on the management of these millions of acres. But who wants to save the money? Do you? Then *you* have to do something about it.

I know of but one electric power corporation that now has a sound Vegetation Management policy. That is Hartford Electric Light Company, now a part of Northeast Utilities, with a policy that dates only from 1965. At present they are transforming the roadside vegetation of their territory in a manner that deserves the widest publicity. Yet they have given no publicity at all to this creditable procedure.

In conclusion, I would say that the green landscape, the Vegetation, is one of the most manageable parts of the Total Environment, manageable at low costs with high long-term values. Yet the available scientific knowledge remains uncommunicated to the rest of society, often because of the short-term private interests of units of that society who are overly vocal with unsound information. To add to the total problem, the Ivory Tower itself can be short of ivory. You see why I asked: "Is there intelligent life on Earth?" What intelligence there is, society should recognize, and use. Such recognition and use are, or should be, the duty of the citizens of a democracy.

CHALLENGES

A symposium that has gathered together an audience of this quality, as well as speakers of eminence like those beside me, should not sink into limbo among those already convinced. Now it would never have occurred to me to challenge anyone openly except for the fact that some brave soul had the courage to title this symposium "Challenge for Survival." Me, I'm a retiring non-controversial individual. Yet it might be wise to place on public record certain specific challenges within the ecological context of a Ninth-Level unity of man-plus-his-total-environment. In doing so, I am fully aware that I may be revealing my own ignorance—that some of my challenges may already have been met and answered. If so, I will be most happy to acknowledge my sin. To keep this part of my address pertinent to this symposium, I will restrict myself to those corporations that have already shown their interest in the subject by appearing on this

program and to a few other organizations that by geography or
activity are closely related.

1. I challenge the Weyerhaeuser Company to formulate,
adopt, and publicize a sound long-term forest land program,
which will not only assure them a reasonable profit from their
timber operations, which will not only consider the long-term
future of the forest as a national asset, which will treat hunting,
fishing, and recreation as more than a hush-puppy for the public,
but also which will serve as a model for the industry in the long-
term handling of such lands for an enduring civilization.

2. I challenge the New York City Department of Parks: (*a*)
to consider parkland as equal in value to adjacent developed land,
including the buildings upon it, and to resist encroachments on
parkland on this basis; (*b*) to preserve its tidal marshes as priceless museum pieces and as economically important integral parts
of the Total Ecosystem, especially in relation to upstream and
offshore fisheries—and not as wasteland suited only for garbage
dumps; (*c*) to cooperate with the schools in making parkland
available for education in ecosystem science, which will teach
our youth that the city is dependent upon the non-city.

3. I challenge the Sinclair Oil Corporation—whose conserva-
tion-oriented advertisements have long deserved high praise—to
formulate, adopt, and publicize a Rightofway Vegetation Management policy for the non-agricultural lands of its pipeline
system that will involve the lowest costs for the most years with
the highest conservation values, and thus to lead the industry,
which at this time shows no evidence of ecologic literacy on the
subject.

4. I challenge the National Audubon Society—which does
have some superbly fine ecologic know-how in the person of its
Vice President for Science: (*a*) to develop the concept of a complete "Natural Area" at its Nature Centers and the role of that
balanced ecosystem in understanding the Total Human Ecosystem and thus to influence other nature centers around the country

which are mostly pegged on studying the birds and the bees and the detrimental influence of man upon them, rather than comprehending the unity of the whole; and (*b*) to publish a new wildlife habitat bulletin for the citizens to supersede the one which not only unintentionally indicts the entire wildlife profession (as indicated by a published letter from the Executive Secretary of the Wildlife Society) but which communicates the deficiencies of that science to the general public.

5. I challenge Consolidated Edison Company: (*a*) to give the public a sound and defensible estimate of the reputedly "high costs" of putting transmission lines underground, not just in terms of construction costs but in the light of the entire long-term period that such underground lines will be in service, and as balanced against the costs of above-ground maintenance and replacement, including hurricane and winter damage; and (*b*) whether or not the transmission lines are underground, I challenge Consolidated Edison to formulate, adopt, and publicize a Rightofway Vegetation Management policy for their transmission and distribution lines that will involve the lowest costs for the most years with the highest scenic, wildlife, and conservation values, and thus to lead the power industry which in the last twenty years has been a notorious destroyer of vegetational resources on private lands under their management.

6. I challenge the Ford Foundation, which has recently completed in the center of the world's largest city a seventeen million dollar structure that is one of the most extraordinary buildings it has ever been my privilege to witness. It contains a garden, one-third of an acre in extent, roofed over at a height of twelve stories; probably the most expensive garden in the entire history of mankind and untaxed since it is part of a non-profit foundation. Curiously, when one stands in this "worth-its-weight-in-gold" garden, one's attention is compellingly directed elsewhere. Through the glass walls in one direction, one admires the Gothic architectural ornamentations of Tudor City (since there is no ornamentation in the Ford building itself; it is surpassingly clean-lined and functional). Through the glass walls in the

other direction one gazes in fascination at twelve stories of offices, by neo-tradition devoid of curtains and shades. For the student of animal behavior, it is similar to being in some underground nature center where there is an exhibit of a subterranean animal whose dens and burrows have been sliced through and sheathed in glass for better observation. As I gazed upward at the almost indecent exposure of this highly social organism, I did feel moved to make one very sober and serious recommendation: that a sign be placed in every office reading "Danger! Miniskirted females are requested to keep away from the edge." But it is because of the garden that I mention the Ford Foundation. There is no question that the Ford Foundation is fully cognizant of the hazardous disruptions to our Human Ecosystems, of the lowered quality of our Total Environment, and of the need for long-term research in Total Ecology. It is my understanding that they are planning to give about four million dollars to a few selected universities to initiate or further their ecology programs. (I am not sure who is kidding whom, but I believe close to one million of that money will go to a university which does not, and does not intend to, hold any legally-preserved Natural Areas. The university does own open space for scientific research, but it expressly reserves the right to dispose of the land if professor-interest or grant-money vanishes from the scene.) Under these circumstances, I challenge the Ford Foundation to use their "garden" for what could become the most extraordinary, controlled-ecosystem project in the history of ecology and in the entire world. Here is a volume of space, one-third of an acre and twelve stories high, completely controlled, air-conditioned, where soil, moisture, carbon, hydrogen, oxygen, plants, and even animals (including birds and small mammals) could be studied and observed as on an island—a project not only of enormous research value, but, in view of its position in the middle of New York City, of stupendous educational significance.

7. I challenge the New York Public Library to prepare, promote, and widely distribute a library on natural resources, ecology, and ecosystem science, one that will not be restricted

because of political or industrial pressures, such as marred certain book lists in other cities after the publication of Rachel Carson's *Silent Spring*.

8. I challenge the New York City education system: (*a*) to use one of its primary schools (kindergarten through sixth grade) as a model, and have it adopt a science program which will present a Total Ecology awareness to its pupils and thus hopefully also to the parents of those children; (*b*) to use one of its high schools (ninth through twelfth grades) as a model, and have it adopt a biology program that will present a Total Ecology awareness to all the students. The text *High School Biology* (Green Version) of the Biological Sciences Curriculum Study is a pioneer in this approach at the Eighth Level, but not at the Ninth Level; (*c*) to use one of the city colleges as a model, and to integrate an ecology teaching program, not as one course in a science department, but as a viewpoint in the entire educational system involving the arts and the humanities as well as the sciences.

9. I challenge the State University of New York to carry on a research program, not just on "natural ecosystems," regardless of how rigorous and sophisticated the computer-technology might appear, and even if a legally-preserved Natural Area is available, but on a Ninth Level Total Human Ecosystem, involving the social sciences as well. I challenge the University to investigate also such theologo-taboo scientific subjects as an investigation of Galbraith's techno-structure (the most pregnant ecologic concept of the decade), the roles of Madison Avenue, Park Avenue, Fifth Avenue, and Wall Street (which have the responsibilities, the potentialities, and, yes, the contemporary factuality in specific instances of playing the role that the aristocracies played at the start of the Classic Age of Greece, in some of the glorious civilizations of the past, and at the birth of this nation two centuries ago); and lastly, I challenge the University to investigate what Philip Wylie has aptly named The Magic Animal, including his sexual nature, his urban and non-urban

nature, his racial nature, and—the greatest taboo of them all—his intelligence.

10. I challenge the Garden Club of America, which represents one of the most tremendous forces in our society—for better or worse. Directly or indirectly the ladies of the G.C.A. control more money than the other half; by having the other half work for them, they have more time at their disposal. The combination is unbeatable and irresistible. The G.C.A. is capable of putting emphasis on beauty, aesthetics, value, quality. One element of the landscape about which they have already shown concern, seen by more citizens than any other in our mobile society, is the roadsides and their greenery. I challenge the G.C.A., operating through one of its member clubs, to develop and effectuate a model policy of Roadside Vegetation Management in cooperation with town, county, and state highway agencies, and with the local telephone and power companies operating roadside utility lines. There would be nothing unprecedented in this move. We read of the initiation of such a plan in the *Bulletin of the Garden Club of America* (45(5):57–60, 1957). Unfortunately, what would have been so helpful to the nation remained on the drawing boards and never became airborne.

11. I challenge the Nature Conservancy, the nation's leading conservation organization devoted primarily to the preservation and study of Natural Areas, to establish a Research Administration policy for ecological studies that is not an insult to the scientists that are giving their volunteer time to the organization. At present, there is no salaried scientist on the staff. Although there is, or was, an Ecological Studies Committee composed of professional ecologists, it is purely advisory in nature. Their opinion is not sought until studies are planned and completed—at times without adequate scientific competence—and the manuscripts submitted for publication. It would seem that these "preservationists" are not "scientists," and any continuance of the present policy not only undermines the morale of those scientists who are volunteering their efforts and in turn damages the image of the

organization in the scientific world, but also that present policy must be reflected in the attitudes of prospective donors of both land and funds to the organization, upon which it is completely dependent.

12. I perforce must challenge our hosts, The New York Botanical Garden, to establish an educational and research program on what is probably their most priceless heritage, the old hemlock forest beside the Bronx River. This forest is *not*—as they have allowed the newspapers to say—a forest primeval untouched since Indian days. In fact, they have let it be overrun by the public, trampled, soil-eroded, and abused in a manner that is scientifically indefensible, and which ecologists have long deplored. On the other hand, this tract, if properly controlled, managed, and studied, could become a truly extraordinary asset to New York City, and to all those who live in and visit it, for both education and research at the Eighth Level of a wild balanced ecosystem, which is in turn demonstrative of the greater complexities of the Human Ecosystem that surrounds it and of which it is a part.

13. And lastly, I challenge the laymen, even in this audience, to do something as citizens. The citizen is the real governing force of our society—for better or worse. He is far freer than the scientist in the university, far freer than the employee in the corporation, far freer than the politician who was voted into office. In the last analysis, it is you the citizen who must accept the Challenge for Survival—and act—or not survive.

CHALLENGE FOR SURVIVAL *Commentary*

by Miles P. Shanahan

The list of organizations challenged by Dr. Egler is most impressive. I'm glad Sterling Forest is not among them!

The balance of man and nature in the ecology and management of land has been a vital concern of Sterling Forest since its inception. We are a part of megalopolis, but we are determined that our forest will never vanish under the bulldozer.

In 1956 City Investing Company acquired a 30-square-mile tract of unspoiled woodlands and hills studded with sparkling mountain lakes and streams. Located near Tuxedo, New York, the forest was virtually unchanged from the days when it was the hunting grounds of the Iroquois Indians.

Sterling Forest is part of our heritage. It has the beauty of the wilderness—something America has sadly neglected in her headlong rush toward progress—and it is also rich in historical lore. In 1707 Queen Anne of England gave royal title to the land to a group of colonists. In 1736 iron ore was discovered in the forest by a representative of the Fifth Earl of Stirling. Lord Stirling subsequently became an aide to General Washington who led his army through the forest on the old Continental Plank Road en route to Newburgh. When the British fleet attempted to sail up the Hudson during the American Revolution it was stopped just short of West Point by the great iron chain forged at Sterling Furnace. Sterling Furnace has been faithfully reconstructed and is now an historic landmark, a part of our history that will be preserved for the generations to come.

The great natural beauty of the forest has also been carefully preserved during the formation of the Sterling Forest Community which comprises education and research centers, residential communities, and cultural and recreational facilities.

Presently situated in Sterling Forest are: Union Carbide Company, with one of the largest privately owned nuclear research facilities in the country; International Nickel Company, which operates a metallurgical research center on the shores of Blue Lake; Reichhold Chemicals Plastics Division; Xicom, Inc.; and International Paper Company, which will complete a $7.5 million corporate research center for occupancy in September 1968.

Several years ago City Investing Company donated a large tract of land to New York University for research and education. The University now has in the forest its Institute of Environmental Medicine and its Laboratory for Experimental Medicine and Surgery in Primates, as well as laboratories for research and study in biology, geology, and ecology. The latter are presently conducting an ecological survey of the Hudson River.

Beside Sterling Lake is the Sterling Forest Conference Center which provides a quiet and beautiful setting for meetings of business, educational, and research organizations.

Three residential areas provide homes for the scientists and for those who enjoy living in natural surroundings. In addition to hiking, swimming, sailing, and fishing for residents, public recreational facilities include Sterling Forest Ski Centre, Sterling Forest Theatre, and Sterling Forest Gardens.

Now, how does Sterling Forest differ from other developed areas?

Stringent regulations on the use of land were established at the outset. Plans for all buildings must be approved by an architectural review committee. Instructions prepared for prospective residents urge, and I quote: "Consider your particular site—its contours, trees, flora, outcroppings of rock, boulders, and so forth, as a primary asset." Before site clearance can begin, the contractor is required to meet with the planning director who insists on the following restrictions, among others:

Only those trees may be cut down that are located in the immediate area of the proposed foundation and driveway and that cannot be saved by reasonable adjustment of the siting plan.

Use of a bulldozer and other mechanical equipment must be restricted to areas absolutely essential to construction or access and in a manner to protect standing trees, rock formations, and other natural settings.

If not removed from the site, boulders excavated during construction must be placed in a manner to enhance the appearance of the site.

If you were to row into the middle of Sterling Lake—and you would have to row because no power boats are permitted—you would see a shore line that looks completely untouched, and it is. Those homes built near the lake must be placed far enough back so that the shore line is undisturbed, and the construction of docks is not allowed. Beauty is maintained, but what is more important, the shoreline ecology is undisturbed.

The factors just mentioned in connection with site and appearance of homes also apply to industry. More important, however, are the strict standards that have been established in relation to industrial waste and the exclusion of anything that might pollute land, air, or water.

In some instances we have enhanced the natural beauty of the forest. Sterling Forest Gardens was originally a large bog area which was drained during 1958 and 1959. The entire area was stripped down to a clay base and then filled in with sand and top soil after an elaborate drainage system was installed. Six connecting lakes were constructed basically as catch basins, but additionally as features of this 125-acre attraction. They are so much a part of the setting that today they have become home to a host of wild birds. Before the gardens opened in 1960, a team of experts from Holland planted a million and a half tulips, hyacinths, daffodils, and other spring-flowering bulbs. Landscape architects designed a series of gardens and background plantings that provide three colorful seasons. For additional interest exotic birds, garden sculpture, and fountains were incorporated in the overall landscaping.

In these brief remarks I have attempted to illustrate how Sterling Forest management has tried in a small way to meet the "Challenge for Survival." From the beginning our objective has been to develop and preserve the natural beauty of the forest while providing an intimate relationship between nature and the living, working, recreational, and cultural environments of its occupants.

We believe we can continue to do this while meeting the economic needs of profit-oriented private enterprise.

Recreation habits and values: implications for landscape quality DAVID LOWENTHAL

"Open space is like virginity," the general manager for state parks in New York City recently remarked. "Once lost, it can never be regained" (Schulman 1968). But this is not entirely true of either. Non-virgins are needed to produce more virgins. And sanitary fill is a prime source of urban open space, if only because the settling of decayed matter precludes building for some time (Stewart 1968). Yesterday's dump is tomorrow's park, or, to paraphrase Wallace Stegner (1967), a man's home is his castle, but his litter belongs to everybody.

Landscape is often seen as a commentary on the human condition (Turner 1966). And as moral metaphors, landscapes are as American as Niagara Falls and redwoods, although not so durable. To New England Puritans the primeval forest was the locus of evil, terror, and witchcraft (Heimert 1953). But in the nineteenth century trees left the devil's domain for a higher place, and what with Arbor Day, Longfellow, Joyce Kilmer, and Smokey the Bear it is a wonder they are ever chopped down.

Moral purpose animates the design of both private and public space. A half-century ago, the United States Department of Agriculture advocated farmstead beautification on the ground that "a home and its surroundings must be attractive in order to be most uplifting to the family, visitors, and passers-by" (1920). Public parks were initially intended to restore the health, improve the character, and elevate the taste of the masses. Surrounded by blight and squalor, urban parks were places deliberately set apart —oases not only of greenery but of the behavior thought appropriate to greenery (Olmsted 1902; Chadwick 1966). "Foul air prompts to vice, and oxygen to virtue," was a truism of park planning in the 1890s (Bould 1894).

Both open space and public opinion still reflect this point of view. Parks scarcely affect urban environment; they often seem pallid, woebegone substitutes for the country, rather than integral aspects of the city scene. The Secretary of Agriculture urges Americans to exchange the "rabbit warrens of the big cities for the fresh air, clean water, and space of the small towns" (Freeman 1967). The latest *Yearbook of Agriculture* insists that "Man needs nature; . . . animals which are forced to live under crowded conditions develop many of the antisocial traits that fill the crime pages of big city newspapers" (Baker 1967, p. 3). The Department of the Interior endorses a Congressman's advice to get "beyond brick and mortar, away from the sound of cities . . . over the hills to God's own country . . . where health and happiness take root . . . where Nature quickens physical, mental and spiritual guidance" (Saylor n. d.).

Such pieties are regularly reiterated, but seldom documented. Some feel that evidence is unnecessary. Open-space preservation "should require no defense," asserts New York City's Open Space Action Committee (1965). Others take refuge in the ineffable: "If the rat and sparrow can learn to live for endless generations in the city, why cannot man?" asks Roger Revelle (1967). Scientists are unable to give us answers, he admits, "but the prophets and poets can."

Every conference on open space "ends up waving the green flag and we salute the Sequoia," a conservation educator complains. "Having saluted the Sequoia all my life, could we not now have a good reason?" When asked whether man had biological and psychological needs for natural experience, he confessed ignorance: "I don't even know whether the question is meaningful" (Brandwein 1968). Meaningful or not, the Department of Agriculture still entreats Americans "to create an outdoor environment that meets the high standards of living within most of our homes," because "the outdoors, too, is our home" (Baker 1967, p. 2).

Is the outdoors in fact "our home," or is it viewed, like purity, as being a rare and precious commodity which to touch is to defile? (Douglas 1966). In surveys I have made, people usually associate open space with arid lands in the Southwest, great expanses and distant horizons, sweeping plains and empty deserts. Cleanness and beauty and freedom predominate, but these places are devoid of human activity. In short, they are meant for reverence, not for recreation; play would pollute them. And so, by analogy, wilderness lovers feel that use desecrates the wild. They urge its preservation as an ideal, all the more precious because rarely, if ever, experienced. "We must ask even those who love the wilderness the most," says a prominent conservationist, "to touch it but seldom, and lightly" (Dasmann 1968).

The outdoor activities of wilderness lovers reflect these ideals. Let me sketch a few traits of the dedicated outdoorsman in order to point up the implications of his behavior for recreation and the landscape.

1. *The outdoorsman observes nature mainly to count and classify.* Birds are watched to be listed; mountains are climbed to be checked off on tally sheets; hikers vie with one another in terms of miles per day and pounds per pack; the Appalachian Trail is walked from end to end as an elite achievement. This is no parody of outdoor interests; such matters are the staple of conversation on many outings.*

2. *The outdoorsman is there to improve himself.* Climbs, hikes, and canoe trips are learning experiences, and instruction is continuous. Sitting around the campfire in the evening, swapping

---

*Donald Culross Peattie (1942) speaks of "those persons with overdeveloped thyroids who walk to set records, who add stones to their packs when climbing mountains and count their steps to calculate how far they have come."

tall tales? Not a bit of it. After the tents are up, supper over, and the gear stowed away, come lessons in knot tying, fiberglassing, life preserving, and equipment buying, or educational films on the finer points of whatever the group has just done or will do next.

3. *The outdoorsman is organized.* In the name of safety everything takes place in groups; teamwork is enforced on gentle trails just as on the steepest mountains. Being alone and getting lost were the height of wilderness experience for nineteenth-century visitors. Thus the painter Thomas Cole in the Catskills: "I was lost . . . I felt a wild and vivid pleasure . . . I shouted, sang, whistled, for the very horror of the thing" (Shepard 1967, p. 182). This is no longer fashionable. Recently I was exhorted to spare no effort in the design of a new edition of a New York area hiking guide "to prevent even one hiker or boy scout from getting lost or caught in the woods after dark."

The outdoorsman enjoys discipline whether he is dishing it out or taking it. When a novice is berated for some minor failure or infraction of the rules, he accepts it meekly; back home, such officious authority would be bitterly resented.

4. *The outdoorsman is a good citizen.* He is eager to be useful and cooperative, takes up the minimum space at campgrounds, is careful not to interfere with other campers, and leaves his site as tidy as a grave. Most other Americans still think of nature, in H. L. Mencken's phrase, as "a place to throw beer cans on Sunday." But such atavism is a source of embarrassment to the serious outdoorsman.

5. *The outdoorsman is a masochist.* His prize recollections involve being attacked by mosquitoes or black flies, drenched by downpours or by falling into rivers, frozen by icy winds or snows, and semi-crippled by extreme exhaustion. Straining muscles and fevered temples are admired as products of "clean work! clean sweat!" but as one devotee confesses (or boasts), "few but the hiker will understand this reverence for exertion" (Sutton and Sutton 1967).* A canoeist put it more baldly, de-

*McKinley (1966) suggests that "the amount of attachment to an area is somewhat in proportion to the amount of actual *physical energy* expended in reaching it."

scribing portaging as "quite simple: just equal parts of masochism and brute force." And although paddling a heavily loaded canoe against the wind "is not exactly the same thing as being a galley slave, it does afford some insight into what that life was like" (Dickenson 1966). Thoroughgoing outdoorsmen even make a fetish of hunger. We are enjoined to emulate Thoreau, who "boiled a handful of rock tripe . . . for more than an hour," and happily announced that "it produced a black puff . . . not positively disagreeable to the palate" (Thoreau 1854).

Discomforts are praiseworthy because they promote intimacy with nature; they also dissuade the tender and unconverted from putting in an appearance. Those who avoid discomfort are dismissed with derision or contempt. Neither age nor condition is an adequate excuse for refusing to suffer. When one outdoorsman noted for his ability to take a beating finally, in his sixties, bought a VW camper, his former cronies shook their heads over this mark of weakness, and the rumor went around that the poor man had slipped so far from the true path as to spend an occasional night in a motel.

Outdoorsmen who endure allow themselves only the most meager comforts and rewards. Novice climbers at the Appalachian Mountain Club winter training school are enticed to the summit by the promise of a lemon and a bite of "glorp"—a bar of pressed raisins, nuts, cereal, and chocolate (Smith 1966). The shivering canoeist scathed by a river mishap is surreptitiously offered the smallest nip of whiskey to warm him.

I do not mean to traduce the experience or to impugn the motives of the outdoorsman. His ascetic traits notwithstanding, he must still be viewed as a recreation seeker, in the sense of Marion Clawson's definition of "recreation" as activity undertaken because one wants to do it (Clawson and Knetsch 1966, p. 6). Nevertheless, his quest for purity and virtue in the outdoors is sharply at odds with the recreation demands and behavior of the great majority.

The general public views the outdoorsman as commendable, but seldom worth emulating. "The urge to 'get back to nature' is an important factor in the lives of increasing numbers of people," the United States Forest Service claims, but its picture of what people do is sharply at variance with this statement. Most campers today are in a hurry; they have a lot to see and a schedule to meet. Equipment and facilities are increasingly luxurious. People with mobile trailers want electrical and water hook-ups rather than fireplaces and tables; they insist on hot and cold running water, showers, flush toilets, and laundry facilities. Indeed, the Forest Service concludes, "visitors seem to be increasingly 'soft.' They don't venture far from their cars. Life in camp, in terms of creature comfort, is not much different from that at home. . . . Even hunters are tending to use motels and restaurants as a base of operations instead of the traditional hunting camp" (USDA 1965). People may like a taste of the outdoors, but they usually do not want to live in it, however briefly.

Above all, most Americans are gregarious. Solitude and silent communion with the great outdoors are the last things the average camper seeks. "My notion of camping," writes Faith Mc-Nulty (1961), "was that we'd . . . manfully make our little home in the wilderness, enjoying the slightly scary pleasures of solitude and independence." But finding no remote spots, they "camped where Americans are supposed to camp"—in state and national parks. "These camps are about as sylvan as Central Park. . . . The whole place was as busy and as merry as the zoo on Sunday. . . . When I mentioned the idea of solitary camping to any of our campmates, they looked puzzled or dismayed. 'You mean you want to camp where there's nobody *around?*' a woman in Zion Park, Utah, asked, in horror. 'Why, I'd be scared simply stiff!' "

The traffic jams at popular national parks are deplored by nature lovers, but the ordinary tourist welcomes the presence of his fellows as a cheery reminder that he is not alone in the wilderness. At the Grand Canyon not one visitor in a hundred ventures below the canyon rim. Few stray from well-worn paths. In Yosemite Valley, Fourth of July campers are estimated at more than eight thousand per square mile: "The damp night air, heavy with a pall of eye-watering smoke, is cut by the blare of transistor radios, the clatter of pots and pans, the roar of a motorcycle, and the squeals of teenagers." Except for the trailers and tents "this might be any city after dark" ("Ah wilderness" 1966).

But this is essentially how many people like parks. Indeed, it is close to what was anticipated by the proponents of our first national park. When N. P. Langford admired Yellowstone Lake in 1870, he predicted it would soon "be adorned with villas and the ornaments of civilized life. . . . The march of civil improvement will reclaim this delightful solitude, and garnish it with all the attractions of cultivated taste and refinement" (Langford 1905).

Daniel Boone is reputed to have felt crowded when he saw the smoke from another cabin. Daniel Boone is dead. Most modern campers do not object to pitching their tents a few feet apart; a campground is said to be full only when you have to use the other fellow's tent pegs. Recreation specialists have conscious or unconscious standards of use intensity that most folk are willing, even happy, to exceed (Clawson and Knetsch 1966, p. 169). After Labor Day, when most campers have left Yosemite, the remainder huddle together to maintain a comfortable feeling of density (Darling and Eichhorn 1967, p. 42).*

Most Americans enjoy nature not to "get away from it all" in the wilderness but to relax in familiar surroundings. The laundromat at Mesa Verde National Park made a lady from Kansas "feel right at home; they even have my favorite detergent" (McKitterick 1965). Modern camping is "the definitive means of getting close to nature . . . without coming to grips with it," according to Gilbert Millstein (1962). "Nobody chews pemmican or gnaws on edible roots and only a handful of eccentrics . . . invite their souls on a bed of boughs." The campers at Groton State Forest, Vermont, all had portable refrigerators and were given stacks of firewood (from logs cut outside the forest). Millstein concluded that their pioneering drive was "a return to the soil—in the fashion . . . of Marie Antoinette pushing sheep around with a gilded crook in the Petit Trianon."

*Lambert (1967) refers to "huddles like defensive circles of covered wagons, even when separate sites remain vacant nearby."

Not even proficient campers eagerly embrace all the rigors of the wilderness. Those interviewed at Glacier and Quetico-Superior national parks expressed pleasure in being able to cope with primitive surroundings, but their conception of "wilderness" was certainly not Aldo Leopold's. They all wanted to preserve primeval nature, but four out of five also asked for more campsites and amenities. They saw no inconsistency in wanting both. For many of them, a forest recreation survey concluded, "wilderness subsumes the existence of picnic tables, wells, toilets, washrooms, and the like" (Bultena and Taves 1961; see also Burch 1964).

The luxuries of camping are easy to lampoon. "Every time I unpack the folding chromium barbecue pit and the dehydrated soup mix, out there under the stars, I say to myself, 'Gil, boy, this is something you can't escape: it's in your blood' " (Atkinson and Searle 1959). All-out primitivism holds little appeal for most Americans. They identify with Huck Finn, who carried as much equipment as possible: a frying pan, a coffeepot, tin cups, a knife, fishhooks, and a gun; his raft was not made of logs but of cut lumber. Hunters in the North Woods may like to identify with hardy eighteenth-century trappers, but bush airlines, light-weight equipment, packaged foods, and bottled gas make modern camping in the far north a luxury proposition. Comfort in camp, sporting operators assert, enhances the guests' enjoyment of the wilderness that surrounds them (Davenport 1962).

"As you grow older," observes a camper, "you learn to tolerate the comforts." Yet discomfort retains a certain cachet. One couple, tired of wet wood, burned pans, and canned rations, realized that they were not pioneers and were pleased about "being honest enough to admit this." They decided to doff their hair shirts and dined in restaurants each evening, but then had to endure the contemptuous disapproval of those who took camping more seriously (Luce 1960). It might not be much of a challenge to survive on packaged food, but a camper ought at least to cook his own meals.

Today a modicum of effort suffices to derive virtue from

nature. A redemptive outdoor experience demands no sacrifice of comfort, no great exertion of muscle; it is a voyage of the mind, a journey through forests that call less for the woodsman's lore than for the impresario's talents. The outdoor church at Table Rock Lake, in the Ozarks, features a biblical *son-et-lumière* entitled "The Shepherd of the Hills" (Ford 1965). On summer evenings in a California national forest campers sit around a simulated log fire listening to nature lore, watching movies, and singing oldtime ballads. After the performance, visitors join in the symbolic ritual of dousing the campfire, while rangers turn the valve that cuts off the gas. No embers smolder to cheer the campers' slumber. Tamed nature has played its passive role, and the modern Prospero returns home refreshed if not exactly reborn.

Every year, however, more and more Americans come back to the outdoors converted to the wilderness mystique. From hedonists and heedless despoilers they become serious-minded amateur ecologists, alive to the risks of pollution, angered by the Corps of Engineers, sworn enemies of the public utilities and lumber companies. And herein lurk new perils to the landscape. An elite minority today guards treasured wilderness against intensive recreational use by the unappreciative majority. But *enlightened* masses will enormously multiply the pressure on recreational land. No longer content to crowd together in Yosemite and Yellowstone, they will fan out to all the wilder reaches of the country. Under such an onslaught, the wilderness is apt to disappear, to be supplanted by fenced preserves and artificial "nature" areas for esoteric outdoor studies.

Intensive use by dedicated outdoorsmen already threatens some areas. In countrysides that easily accommodate individual ramblers, fishermen, and hunters, hiking clubs may be anathematized; organized recreation is apt to endanger or foreclose covenants with landowners allowing rights-of-way across private property. A dozen well-booted hikers as a body are more likely to disturb the vegetation and compact the soil of a trail than as many sauntering individual wayfarers (Darling and Eichhorn

1967, p. 40; Shepard 1967, pp. 258–269). The organized group is also a visual, often an aural, outrage to the resident population and lends to the landscape an unwelcome impression of public ownership. The outdoorsman's environmental needs are thus both special and exclusive; coexistence with residential land use is almost out of the question. Both his tastes and his impact on the land push him away from lived-in countryside to wilderness reserves.

It is well to recall that the virtues of the wild were formerly seen in quite another light. Americans used to enjoy the wilderness, if at all, mainly to imagine how much better it would look when the forests were replaced by fruitful fields and teeming towns (Nash 1967). Not until the nineteenth century did James Fenimore Cooper and the Hudson River school of painters provide a true wilderness esthetic. Even so, it was the association of wilderness with ruins that endeared it to many Americans. Dead trees were admired as analogues of European architectural relics, and ruined arches were placed up and down the Hudson to enhance the effect of nature.

The Catskills and Adirondacks were later esthetically outclassed by western landscapes more stupendous and more evocative of human associations. The stratified sedimentary and volcanic rock formations of the West moved visitors profoundly because they reminded them of ruins of great cities, castles, temples, and other monuments of ancient civilization. "One could almost imagine," wrote the geologist Frederick V. Hayden after his Yellowstone expedition of 1871, "that the idea of the Gothic style of architecture had been caught from such carvings of Nature" (Bryant 1872; see also Shepard 1956–57).* These architectural qualities made Yellowstone famous and help to account for its popularity ever since.

It was such curiosities, more than the primeval wilderness, that

*At the same time, Americans were fond of viewing these wonders of nature, by contrast with their artificial European counterparts, as symbols of freedom from aristocratic oppression (Turner 1884).

inspired Congress to consecrate the first national park as a "pleas-
uring ground for the use and enjoyment of the people." The
very word "park" suggests the role originally foreseen for places
like Yellowstone and Yosemite. Both the private landscape parks
of the eighteenth century and the urban public parks of the
nineteenth were consciously contrived as places for "congre-
gated human life under glorious and necessarily artificial conditions" (Olmsted 1902, p. 49). Park landscapers from "Capability" Brown and Humphry Repton to Andrew Jackson Downing
and Frederick Law Olmsted did not aim at imitating, much less
preserving, nature but at selecting from and improving on it.
Unlike natural landscapes, parks were dominated by grassy
lawns and groves of big trees free of undergrowth and often
contained ornamental structures and ruins, real or make-believe.

Only within the past generation has our emphasis shifted from
the tangible enjoyment of spectacular features, natural or artificial, to a more abstract appreciation of untouched wilderness.
But if intensive use causes landscape maintenance problems at the
Yellowstone and Yosemite campgrounds, visitor impact presents
potentially graver hazards in such areas as Rocky Mountain
National Park or even the Everglades and the Olympics. Far
from "parklike" to begin with, these fragile ecosystems can
hardly survive mass recreation; as Dasmann (1968) has said,
they may have been better off when nobody cared about them.
The overcrowded wilderness, like the neglected urban park, is
the fruit of distinctions increasingly and unwisely drawn between wild and tame, natural and artificial, countryside and megalopolis.

"Civics as an art," remarked the pioneer city planner Patrick
Geddes (1904), has to do "not with imagining an impossible
no-place where all is well, but with making the most and the best
of each and every place, and especially of the city in which we
live." We cannot achieve this by hankering after some distant or
exclusive paradise and abandoning all else as beyond hope. It is
not only in the wilderness that we escape the tensions of civilized

life; man-made environments can also be salubrious. To regard everything used as irretrievably spoiled is, moreover, to relegate the wilderness itself to a museum.

City dwellers have come to believe nature can be found only in unspoiled forests and distant mountains. But nature is in fact all around them—in their own backyards and streets, vacant lots and waterfronts. We need to foster an appreciation of nature in all its guises, humanized as well as wild, near as well as far, intimate as well as grand, transplanted as well as preserved.

The once-in-a-lifetime wilderness experience, the two-week cross-country jaunt, the Sunday jog around the reservoir: these are too rare to sustain a real appreciation of nature, even when supplemented by sumptuous picture books of primeval areas. The aspects of the outdoors that people care about most effectively are those with which they are familiar; to love at a distance is not enough.

REFERENCES

"Ah wilderness." 1966. *Wall Street Journal*, June 24. Quoted in Warren A. Johnson. Over-use of the national parks. *National Parks Magazine* 41 (October 1967): 4. See also *Forbes*, July 15, 1966, pp. 39–42.

Atkinson, Alex, and Ronald Searle. 1959. *By rocking-chair across America*. New York, Funk & Wagnalls, p. 21.

Baker, John A. 1967. The outdoors is for all of us. In *Outdoors USA, The Yearbook of Agriculture 1967*, Washington, D.C.

Bould, E. R. 1894. Park area and open spaces. Quoted in Ian R. Stewart. Parks, progressivism and planning. *Landscape Architecture* 58 (1968): 201.

Brandwein, Paul. 1968. (Remarks at a roundtable discussion at the Research Center for Outdoor Needs (RECON), New York, January 26.)

Bryant, William Cullen (editor). 1872. *Picturesque America; or, the land we live in*. New York, D. Appleton and Company, Volume I, p. 300.

Bultena, Gordon L., and Martin J. Taves. 1961. Changing wilderness images and forestry policy. *Journal of Forestry* 59:169.

Burch, William R., Jr. 1964. Two concepts for guiding recreation management decisions. *Journal of Forestry* 62: 707–712.

Chadwick, George F. 1966. *The park and the town: public landscape in the 19th and 20th centuries.* New York, Frederick A. Praeger.

Clawson, Marion, and Jack L. Knetsch. 1966. *Economics of outdoor recreation.* Baltimore, The Johns Hopkins Press.

Darling, F. Fraser, and Noel D. Eichhorn. 1967. *Man and nature in the national parks: reflections on policy.* Washington, D.C., The Conservation Foundation.

Dasmann, Ray. 1968. *A different kind of country.* New York, The Macmillan Company, p. 24.

Davenport, Arthur. 1962. Soft life in the Canadian wilds. *The New York Times,* July 12, Sect. 10.

Dickenson, James R. 1966. The responsive canoe. In *America outdoors: a report in depth on the nation's natural heritage,* ed. by Edwin A. Roberts, Jr., Silver Spring, Maryland, *The National Observer,* pp. 129 and 134.

Douglas, Mary. 1966. *Purity and danger: an analysis of concepts of pollution and taboo.* London, Routledge & Kegan Paul, pp. 162–163.

Ford, Edsel. 1965. Campers' church. *The New York Times,* June 6, Sect. 10.

Freeman, Orville L. 1967. Quoted in Roy Reed. First lady hails good rural life and praises Minnesota projects as 4-day tour starts. *The New York Times,* September 21, p. 40.

Geddes, Patrick. 1904. City development: a study of parks, gardens, and culture-institutes. Quoted in Chadwick, *op. cit.,* p. 227.

Heimert, Alan. 1953. Puritanism, the wilderness and the frontier. *New England Quarterly* 26: 361–382.

Lambert, Darwin. 1967. The national parks experience. *National Parks Magazine* 41 (May): 5.

Langford, Nathaniel Pitt. 1905. *Diary of the Washburn expedition to the Yellowstone and Firehole Rivers in the year 1870.* N.p., pp. 96–97.

Luce, William P. 1960. How to rough it with a touch of elegance. *The New York Times,* June 5, Sect. 10.

McKinley, Donald. 1966. Psychology of wilderness. *Mazama* 48 (13): 34.

McKitterick, Nathaniel M. 1965. Perking up the nation's parks. *New Republic*, September 18, p. 15.

McNulty, Faith. 1961. Department of amplification. Letter of February 2, 1961, in *The New Yorker*, February 25, pp. 94–95.

Millstein, Gilbert. 1962. Murmuring pines and martinis. *The New York Times Magazine*, July 29, pp. 23–26.

Nash, Roderick. 1967. *Wilderness and the American mind*. New Haven, Yale University Press, pp. 59–60.

Olmsted, Frederick Law. 1902. *Public parks*. Brookline, Massachusetts.

Open Space Action Committee. 1965. *Stewardship*. New York, p. 13.

Peattie, Donald Culross. 1942. The joy of walking. *The New York Times Magazine*, April 5. Quoted in Aaron Sussman and Ruth Goode. *The magic of walking*. New York, Simon and Schuster, 1967, p. 296.

Revelle, Roger. 1967. Outdoor recreation in a hyper-productive society. *Daedalus* 96(4): 1175.

Saylor, John P. N.d. Quoted in *Man . . . an endangered species?* United States Department of the Interior *Conservation Yearbook* No. 4, 1968, Washington, D.C., p. 97.

Schulman, Seymour J. 1968. In *The New York Times*, March 4, p. 49.

Shepard, Paul. 1956–57. Dead cities in the American West. *Landscape* 6(2): 25–28.

Shepard, Paul. 1967. *Man in the landscape: a historic view of the esthetics of nature*. New York, Alfred A. Knopf.

Smith, Clyde H. 1966. Hiking to "glorp" and glory. *The New York Times*, January 23, Sect. 10, p. 27.

Stegner, Wallace. 1967. The people vs. the American continent. *Vermont History* 35: 181.

Stewart, George R. 1968. *Not so rich as you think*. Boston, Houghton Mifflin Company, pp. 88–89.

Sutton, Ann, and Myron Sutton. 1967. *The Appalachian Trail*. Philadelphia, J. B. Lippincott Company, pp. 125–126.

Thoreau, Henry David. 1854. Journal, March 9. Quoted in Eddie W. Wilson. The gastronomic wilderness. *Living Wilderness* (Summer 1961), 20–23.

Turner, A. Richard. 1966. *The vision of landscape in renaissance Italy*. Princeton, Princeton University Press, p. 212.

Turner, Frederick Jackson. 1884. Architecture through oppression. *University Press*, Volume 15, June 21. Quoted in *American Historical Review* 72(1966): 45–46.

United States Department of Agriculture. 1920. Beautifying the farmstead. *Farmers' Bulletin No. 1087*, Washington, D.C., pp. 2–3.

United States Department of Agriculture. 1965. Outdoor recreation in the national forests. *Agriculture Information Bulletin No. 301*, Washington, D.C., pp. 27–30.

CHALLENGE FOR SURVIVAL *Commentary*
by Charles C. Morrison, Jr.

Because I am a fellow geographer and a former colleague at the American Geographical Society, it would be surprising if I did not agree with some of Dr. Lowenthal's contentions. At the same time, our past and present circumstances make it no less unusual that I do not agree with everything he has said.

As is his custom, Dr. Lowenthal has pieced together—artfully —a provocative and pleasant potpourri. His special interests in the study of environmental perception find some ready targets in the views of open space and outdoor recreation held by various segments of our society. There is no question that our attitudes towards nature and our behavior in it are "sharply at odds with everyday life." It is important to dissect these attitudes if we expect to exercise effective control over the quality of our environment. The process of developing public policy is very complex. Certainly the rationalization of our attitudes and behavior should be accomplished with thoroughness and sophistication as a part of the process, and the resulting knowledge should be understood widely.

I understand that our rules in this symposium permit a commentator to speak about everything except the subject paper—if he chooses to do this. Although it is tempting to take advantage of this prerogative, I am going to concentrate mainly on the issues raised by Dr. Lowenthal. Also, I have chosen to regard all of his remarks quite seriously, just to avoid treading the cavalier path.

Dr. Lowenthal's quotations, references, and examples add spice and sparkle to his presentation. But sometimes they seem to have been selected and interpreted with little regard for the full meaning of the original material or situation. In some instances, the result is caricaturization. This is the principal basis for any disagreement I have with him.

As a starting point, it is worth noting that one of the swords wielded by Dr. Lowenthal cuts more sharply with the edge he didn't use. The Stegner quotation—"Man's home is his castle, but his litter belongs to everybody"—properly characterizes the root, if not the seed, of many of our environmental problems: over-population. A man's progeny indeed belongs to everyone! Birth control and family planning are the keystones of any program for environmental control.

The naïveté ascribed—both directly and indirectly—to planners and administrators who have open-space preservation and recreation responsibilities is unfortunate if one takes the view that such naïveté does a disservice to a cause shared by us all. This view of practitioners is lopsided, but there also is enough truth in it to make the matter worth discussing.

Some practitioners have been exposed to a wide range of recreational attitudes and behavior, and some have been involved in original research in this field. Some, seeing no polarization between academically derived and applied knowledge, not only are quite up-to-date on research matters but also exhibit considerable flexibility in moving between academic and government circles.

On the other hand, the rapid development of the field of outdoor recreation resource planning and coordination has brought many people into a new situation they are not equipped to handle. It is going to take time for this to shake down. Although many recruits for this field are being drawn from disciplines which provide a background for an integrative view of environment, a modern understanding of the communication requirements of public administration and the planning process, the people in key positions often are alumni of the old guard resource management schools. Some of these people are out of tune with current thought and practice in planning and intergovernmental relations. They have not grown with their profession. Obviously this is not the kind of leadership that will attract, hold, and train an able staff. It probably will take a decade or more before this situation begins to improve.

The other aspect of the problem is very much related to that of personnel, but it pertains to concepts and techniques. Clichés and jargon abound in outdoor recreation planning at present.

Thus, we hear mumbling about the need to be "people-oriented" and chanting about "supply, demand, and needs," with almost no understanding of the meaning of these words or the concepts behind them. Much of this terminology has been carried over from the intricate and much-criticized cost-benefit methodology built up to justify water storage projects.

Considering the lack of articulation in these matters generally, it is not surprising that an elaborate, and largely worthless, system of statistical manipulation has been promulgated as the cornerstone of outdoor recreation planning. This involves subtracting "supply" from "demand" in order to arrive at a quantification of "needs." These inane calculations, which lack any conceptual grounding and compound error with inaccuracy at every step, are justified on the grounds that "we have nothing better." Doing nothing is not necessarily the only alternative to spending inordinate amounts of staff time and computer time grinding out worthless statistics. Since no one really has any faith in this mumbo-jumbo, its perpetuation accomplishes only a further muddying of the comprehensive planning waters to the benefit of the ad hoc decision makers. It denies progress toward true understanding of the planning process and development of a sound conceptual and methodological framework for outdoor recreation resource allocation.

Now let's go back to the subject of virginity. I agree with our manager of state parks for New York City, if only out of sympathy for the magnitude of his task of superimposing a state park system on the most intensively developed city in the nation—all without incorporating any existing city park into his plans. As he said, open space cannot be regained once it is lost. After our land resources are developed, our economic system is weighted in favor of keeping them developed far into the future. Loss of highly developed or artificial open space is bad enough, but if natural values were associated with the lost open space, we might as well think in terms of the geologic time scale before expecting the developed land to revert to its natural state.

Dozens of square miles of parkland on the periphery of Brooklyn or Staten Island, obtained by the sanitary landfill method, can't serve the function of a Central or Prospect Park or of small neighborhood parks such as Morningside Park in the Columbia University area. The great tragedy is that while it is extremely difficult to gain any new truly functional open space in these intensively developed urban areas, the existing spaces are subject to continuing encroachment by high-minded people who "desperately" need a route for a highway or a site for so-called worthy projects such as restaurants, elementary schools, relocation housing, or university gymnasiums.

It is axiomatic that open space should be functional. None of us would disagree with Dr. Lowenthal's concluding remarks that open space and natural environment should be part of our everyday experience. This has been one of the main theses of the planning and conservation movements. The reports of the Outdoor Recreation Resources Review Commission stressed this. The Open Space Action Committee, the Sierra Club, The American Society of Planning Officials, and many other organizations subscribe wholeheartedly to the idea. The policies of most large-scale public and private development and redevelopment programs now reflect this. The goal is being achieved in some areas. But much remains to be done.

The real issues lie not in whether open space should be functional, but in the nature of the functions, the design and management, and the costs. Man's effect on his environment has been sweeping and complete, however haphazard and ill-conceived. In one way or another even the most remote wilderness has been affected by our technology. No landscape feature on earth can withstand the force of our present technologic and engineering capabilities. Increasing public management and planning for all of our resources are essential if the quality of our environment is to be protected from further exploitation and despoilation. At the same time remedial action is required for damage already done.

It is a specious argument that "nature" or "wilderness" or parkland must be preserved for its own sake. The very act of setting aside land to be managed for wilderness purposes denies this.

Natural areas are preserved for man—for his benefit, and, within
the limitations of management goals, for his use. This is as true
of a public city park as it is for privately owned resources or
for the most remote and extensively undeveloped public lands.
The degree of development and use or multiple use—the dichot-
omous "preservation vs. mass use" argument—becomes irrelevant
when it is realized that *all* resources must be managed. It is only
management objectives and their related practices that should
differ from one type of resource situation to the next.

We need a great diversity of open-space types to match the
catholic outdoor tastes of a diverse population. Restoration of
the boat house in Prospect Park is just as important as purchase
of some of the in-holdings in our western national forests and
vice versa. Democratically determined public policy does not
imply an ever narrowing homogenization of preferences. Cater-
ing only to mass tastes, if carried to its extremes, would reduce
our options, one by one, to a common cultural denominator.
There is enough of this already as a result of mass production of
goods, services, and communications, without giving the trend
more active public assistance. Our public policy should be one of
foreclosing the fewest possible alternatives for the future and
striving to develop some new ones.

Castigation of both those who partake in a "quest for purity
and virtue" and those who enjoy creature comforts while rec-
reating in the outdoors may be an exercise which, Dr. Lowenthal hopes, will strike some spark of illumination. For myself, I
see nothing unusual, in light of our being accustomed to electric
dishwashers, baseboard hot water heat, and flush toilets, in a
desire for comfort on the part of the majority of recreationists.
Why shouldn't we cluster tent-peg-to-tent-peg around the total-
electric modern rest rooms in the latest Mission 66 campground?
We have sought these comforts since the time when groups of
men huddled around campfires in caves. Many of the people who
enjoy flocking to intensively developed campgrounds have
small children; they require conveniences. Such families probably could not afford to see the wonders (or "freaks") of nature

that are enshrined in our national parks if they did not resort to camping.

If our interpretive and educational programs are going well, these people—and our total environment—will be much better for their experience. As they grow more accustomed to the outdoors and acquire some new skills, perhaps many will venture from the campfire into the less-populated hinterlands, thereby unlocking new doors of appreciation and understanding of environmental relationships for themselves. It may well be that a little knowledge is a dangerous thing, as Dr. Lowenthal contends. On the other hand, there is the prospect of gaining a few more people who will become actively involved in environmental problems and their solution. We can't all leap into the breach as full-blown men for all seasons.

At the same time, I also see nothing unusual in the excesses of those whose devotion to wilderness and the "pure" experience is in sharp contrast to their everyday experiences. I am not sure that their "masochism" in the outdoors, as Dr. Lowenthal puts it, is not a reaction to the severe physical and psychological stresses imposed by our urban environments. Furthermore, it seems to me that extremists who place a very high personal value on natural environment—the proverbial little old ladies in tennis shoes who lie down in front of the bulldozers—are a wholly necessary element in our society as long as we have those who with equally single-purposed ardor direct our overwhelming technology and engineering talent with utter insensitivity for the landscape and the ecologic well-being of present and future residents of this planet. Would that more of our confrontation politics took this form! But such action-packed extremism preferably should originate in an ever-enlarging group of informed environmentalists. Reactionary misanthropes can do more harm than good.

Although the shortage of money in the central cities relative to burgeoning demands for public funds has caused a serious deterioration in the maintenance and operation of city parks, it is far from being universally true that these old parks raise "in most minds the image of a formal area, empty or partly filled with rather disreputable characters." Anyone who believes this should go out and take a look at the parks. People care about their city parks. They need them and are using them as never before.

As to the national parks, it is true that they were established to preserve the "curiosities" in them and "not to adore the primeval wilderness." The parks then were viewed as "artificial creations" and not as natural areas. But this view has changed, as Dr. Lowenthal points out. Increased use has precipitated the development of new management policies aimed at controlling the use of each park in such a way as to avoid damage to fragile natural features. For some time an elaborate master planning program has been underway in each park to help accomplish this. Roadway construction, signs and informational materials, and intensive-use areas all are designed and located to control use in appropriate fashion. In addition, a strong movement is in progress to get the areas of intensive use out of the parks altogether and into adjoining national forests and public lands. This specialized form of regional planning is now quite advanced.

As touched on earlier in these remarks, one of the burs under the saddle of all who have a professional or lay interest in environment lies in the problem of identifying priorities and alternative uses for resources. The difficulty relates to the fact that all of our needs are quite relative; very few of them are absolute. (There are some absolutes pertaining to our natural environments which are not yet in sharp focus.) The theories and techniques of welfare economics planning are becoming more sophisticated—so much so that the complex results often exceed the understanding of the general public and of the legislators who must respond. These matters can be simplified and clearly articulated, as illustrated by the following example.

During the past few years the first nationwide plan for outdoor recreation has been in preparation in the Department of the Interior. This is due to be released soon as the first major sequel to the 1962 report of the Outdoor Recreation Resources Review Commission. In working on that plan, we sifted thousands of pieces of information and developed many interesting clues as to what kind of open space is "needed" and where it is needed. Here is an elementary example of the kind of information that was grist for the program mill: when we learned through the 1965 National Recreation Survey (Department of the Interior 1968) that only 27 per cent of the non-white population swim whereas 50 per cent of white persons do so, the conclusions about priorities and needs for swimming facilities relative to our current economic and social turmoil were obvious (Morrison 1966). It is clear that equal opportunity in outdoor recreation is as much of a national goal as it is in other related areas of our existence and that these matters are urgent.

The old "10 acres per thousand" rule-of-thumb is the classic example of the kinds of straws for which some recreation planners still grasp in trying to communicate priorities and needs. When planners say they need 10 acres of recreation land for every thousand persons in a community, they *may* know that this is an oversimplification. But they *should* know that the only way to properly evaluate community open space and recreation needs is through a thorough and articulate analysis of existing and potential resources. They *should* know that the priorities they recommend should bear a strong relation to current and anticipated economic and social conditions as well as reflect the habits and preferences of various elements in the community, including those who may not be very vocal. They *should* know that this type of planning has to be done with full recognition of a wide range of federal, state, and local programs, laws, and financial conditions. They *should* know that continuous adaptation of plans and programs is required as new information becomes available and as skills and tools are sharpened. Most planners do all of this, albeit with varying degrees of sophistication and articulation.

But, just try to explain the complexities of planning at a public meeting full of discordant factions! It is much simpler—and more effective—to say "we need 10 acres per thousand." Use of clichés of this kind does not mean that most planners do not strive to develop, at the same time, a better public understanding of all considerations that should go into a plan or program. The planner rides parallel tracks in this regard, hoping they will converge on the horizon.

Identification and preservation of historic places and structures, scenic areas and sites, natural features, cultural landmarks, and architecture of high quality also are simplistic devices used by planners to focus public attention on specific issues and elements of the landscape. They know full well that this too is an oversimplification of the complexity and interrelatedness of environment. Individual elements of our environment are enshrined for perhaps the same reasons that academicians approach the universe of knowledge along innumerable, but separate, disciplinary avenues. It is a matter of both necessity and convenience.

Environmental quality, natural beauty, and beautification are new and vague terms; all require considerable explaining to a skeptical public. Let's take "beautification" for a start. The ". . . present vogue for beautification" is not just skin deep (Lowenthal 1968). Rather it is misunderstood. It is true that a few petunias along Pennsylvania Avenue are not harbingers of a design renaissance. Nor are people suddenly going to wake up some morning and demand a better environment. To be fair, however, Mrs. Johnson's personal involvement in environmental problems has extended far beyond elementary landscaping projects in the Capital, although the importance of her influence there should not be minimized either. Her sincere attention to numerous conservation, planning, and design problems has served to stimulate many actions and programs. This influence has been felt throughout the country.

But Mrs. Johnson did not start the "new conservation," the movement for quality in all aspects of environment, both natural and man-made. She merely hung the prissy misnomer of "beautification" on certain elements of it. Actually, the threads of conservation and planning have been running toward a more integrated approach to management of the total environment for a long time. This has been supported by long-term trends in the physical and social sciences. (Geography in the 1920s at the

University of Chicago already was considered to be a study of human ecology.) The threads were joined in the late 1950s through the creation of the Outdoor Recreation Resources Review Commission by President Eisenhower. Presidents Kennedy and Johnson carried the movement forward.

Quality in environment is a goal to be sought on a continuing basis through a citizenry with an increasingly real understanding and appreciation of environment. The educational requirements for this are stupendous. Education for environmental control must be carried on not only through the schools and colleges but through every available medium. Ignorance of environmental problems and their solutions no longer can be afforded. As Dr. Lowenthal said at another symposium: "As long as landscapes are considered either ideal *or* hopeless, as long as decisions involving environmental quality are seen in terms of polar opposites, little progress can be made either in changing public views or in improving the livability of our milieu" (Lowenthal 1966).

In New York State one of the principal means by which we will encourage environmental awareness is through the creation of action groups, of broad-based membership in all municipalities across the state, stressing partnership between private and public interests. These environmental commissions are expected to have a focal point at the county level, in a council. At the state level they will receive support from the New York State Natural Beauty Commission. We already have begun a scenic roads program, with a committee in every county, as a start in developing this kind of grass-roots involvement.

We also need a better organizational and functional focus at the national level. Natural beauty—the "new conservation"—may not keep the momentum it has gained unless such a focal point is developed. Most states held Governor's Conferences on Natural Beauty following the 1965 White House Conference, and some, like Maryland with its Environmental Trust, have followed New York's lead by establishing a legislatively created body to foster local action.

But, if we are to have proper national leadership for the kind of evaluation and control of the environment that is embodied in the spirit of this conference, there is a distinct need for a National Environmental Trust.

The President's Council on Recreation and Natural Beauty, with the Vice President as permanent Chairman and staff services provided by the Bureau of Outdoor Recreation in the Department of the Interior, represents an important step along the way to appropriate national representation for environmental quality. The recent bills in Congress for a Council of Environmental Advisors or an Environmental Commission or Institute have heated up the debate about organizational requirements for the task ahead. Whatever the next step, one thing is clear: the agency that is established should have the staff capability and the authority that is necessary to carry out its mission.

REFERENCES

Lowenthal, David. 1966. Environmental quality in a growing economy. *Resources for the Future* (essays from the sixth Forum). Baltimore, Johns Hopkins Press.

Lowenthal, David. 1968. The American scene. *The Geographical Review* 58(1):61–68.

Morrison, Charles C., Jr. 1966. A national survey of outdoor recreation participation and preferences. Paper presented at the Annual Meeting of the Association of American Geographers, Toronto. 10 pp.

United States Department of the Interior. 1968. *The 1965 survey of outdoor recreation activities.* Washington, D.C., Bureau of Outdoor Recreation, 210 pp. (multilith).

Photo by W. Cadzow: Chinook over Calgary
(Alberta, Canada).

AIR

Metropolitan air layers and pollution HELMUT E. LANDSBERG

Air is a necessity to man's survival. It is seemingly in endless supply. But in fact it is an inherited resource. It is part of the planetary endowment. Only minute parts are added or subtracted by present natural phenomena. It is a valuable and essential element in sustaining life on earth.

On this premise, contamination of the air by foreign matter is serious indeed. The facts of the case have been presented again and again. Yet they still require repetition.

Let's start from the beginning. Air, essentially a mixture of oxygen, nitrogen, argon, carbon dioxide, and a few other minor constituents, in its natural state is very pure. But it always must have carried a small amount of dust from blowing soil and sand storms in deserts and some salt from evaporated sea water. Nature used these particles to good advantage as centers of condensation for cloud droplets and as nuclei for freezing of ice crystals. These are important for precipitation processes, which in turn wash out these contaminants. Occasionally a volcanic eruption, a fire caused by lightning, or an invasion of cosmic dust from a meteoritic shower may have raised the content of foreign admixtures to the air, but natural processes usually eliminate such material rapidly.

When man, the artisan, began to take over the earth, things

Reprinted from *Garden Journal* 19(2): 54–57, 1969; lightly edited.

started to change. He tamed the fire to his use without taming the smoke. Thus, from an early date of civilization man began to contaminate the air. As he moved into cool latitudes heat became a necessity, and the combustion processes multiplied. Hand in hand with the so-called progress of society went urbanization. Denser and denser settlements began. Smoke from the habitations soon became a nuisance, especially after coal replaced wood as a principal fuel. Evelyn (1661) complained about it over three hundred years ago. But in his day the problem was confined to a few localities. Most of the yet limited population of the world lived in rural environs.

The Industrial Revolution of last century also marked a turning point, perhaps I should say an up-turning point, in the history of atmospheric pollution. In staccato fashion, mills, smelters, electric generating plants, chemical plants, and eventually refineries added to the atmosphere a welter of foreign substances that would take an hour just to enumerate. Cities grew, and growth multiplied space-heating. Goods and people had to be transported, and the railroads and ships added their odious effluents to the mixture.

But worse was still to come. This was the conquest of transportation by the internal combustion engine. Just as the forest of belching smokestacks, the automobile became the manifestation not only of affluence but also of effluence. It was joined by the smoke-trailing jet engine; and the end is not yet in sight. At the same time the agglomeration of an ever-expanding population in cities continued; and the end is not yet in sight here either.

This is a good place to establish a bench-mark by stating the mid-century estimate of pollutant quantities and their sources for the United States, as given by the Public Health Service and reproduced in the following table.

This does not include some major components. Carbon dioxide, for example, is not a health hazard, but may have important climatic effects, as we shall see. Nor should the fact that many contaminants are lumped in the minor category "Others" blind us as regards their importance. This group contains such ob-

Major sources of air pollution in the United States
(millions of tons/year)

Contaminant:	Carbon monoxide	Sulfur oxides	Hydro-carbons	Nitrogen oxides	Parti-cles	Others	Totals
Sources:							
Transportation	66	1	12	6	1	<1	86
Industry	2	9	4	2	6	2	25
Generation of electricity	1	12	<1	3	3	<1	20
Heating	2	3	1	1	1	<1	8
Refuse disposal	1	<1	1	<1	1	<1	4
Total	72	25	18	12	12	4	143

noxious substances as fluorides, lead compounds, and beryllium, which have adverse health effects.

Most of these contaminants originate in metropolitan areas. The past practice has been to let nature take its course. That means we have placed reliance on atmospheric events to disperse, dilute, and eventually eliminate the contaminants. Let us take a look here at the natural processes that operate. Most important for dispersal is the wind. If ventilation is strong, the pollutants are quickly diluted by fresh air streaming through the cities and becoming widely dispersed throughout the atmosphere. This process is particularly efficient if the vertical temperature stratification of the atmosphere permits vertical motions and turbulence. This is usually the situation when the temperature decreases rapidly with altitude. On the other hand, very commonly the temperature may decrease only slightly with height or even be warmer aloft than near the surface. This inversion condition prevents vertical mixing, and only a thin surface layer of air will participate in the dilution of the pollutants. They are essentially trapped. This condition is frequent at night when the earth's surface radiates heat and cools the adjacent air layers more than the air in the free atmosphere. Very often these conditions are coupled with weak winds, so that two natural elements combine to aggravate the pollution problem. In midday both wind and temperature stratification are more commonly favorable to dispersal. Yet some times, in sluggishly moving high-pressure systems, inversion conditions (often coupled with general downdrafts in the atmosphere and low wind speeds) may last for several days, and then pollutants can accumulate to dangerous levels. These meteorological conditions have caused all the major air-pollution catastrophes (Meuse Valley, Donora, London). These conditions, contrary to some popular opinion, are not infrequent. In our regions they can be expected at least once or twice a year, lasting for periods up to a week's duration.

Less known, but rather important for an assessment of pollution danger, is the fact that at least 40 per cent of the nights develop inversion conditions which are often coupled with weak winds.

Another ingredient of the weather acts importantly and that is sunshine. Agreeable although it may feel to most of us, it, too, has adverse effects in the air-pollution picture. It causes photochemical reactions in the basic pollutants. These reactions can cause a relatively innocuous pollutant to become highly irritant. The formation of ozone is an example. This tri-atomic oxygen is not only highly damaging to many ornamental and crop plants, it also causes irritation of the mucous membranes in humans. The list of other compounds produced in a polluted atmosphere by solar radiation is also formidable. These are essentially the causes of the photochemical smogs in Los Angeles. But, although this city has been by habit exclusively identified with such smog, it is by no means unique. In fact, eastern cities have photochemical smogs too.

Turning to particulates, we all know that gravity has an important effect, especially on the larger particles. They fall out. Every housewife is well aware of this effect. And the amounts of fallout over major cities are truly staggering. However, this eliminates only the largest particles, usually over 3 to 5 microns in diameter. The smaller particles float with the air and may stay in suspension for a long time. These are the same particles which penetrate the lungs, where according to their nature and toxicity they may do all kinds of harm. This atmospheric flotsam has a curious relation to atmospheric condensation. In small numbers it induces the formation of droplets which, because of their relatively large size, promote the fallout and cleansing process. Yet, if too many of these small particles compete for the available water vapor in the atmosphere, they may actually hinder the formation of larger drops which are essential in precipitation processes. Here we encounter a situation where human waste products can have a substantial but unplanned and unwanted influence on a natural event. It is one of the possible long-range consequences of air pollution. On the whole, though, natural rain formation still has the upper hand and helps in the elimination of many air pollutants.

For one of the most insidious pollutants, sulfur dioxide, high atmospheric moisture promotes hydrolization and the formation of sulfuric acid. In foggy weather situations with stagnant, stable air this is one of the elements causing respiratory distress. It is undoubtedly responsible for deaths and illnesses in acute air-pollution situations. The sulfur compounds also have led to widespread plant damage and are the direct cause of the elimination of lichens from the inner cities and industrial areas. The extent of the so-called lichen desert is usually a very sensitive criterion of how far pollution has spread in a metropolitan area. There is also little doubt that the interaction of the sulfur dioxide with the atmospheric water vapor causes low visibilities, which are at least a nuisance for air traffic. At the Los Angeles airport, for instance, visibility is reduced by one mile for every 25 thousand barrels of fuel oil consumed per day. Most students of the air-pollution problem are convinced that sulfur dioxide should remain one of the first targets for elimination at the source. Those of us who have artistic concerns may also contemplate with sadness, in this connection, that the sulfur-dioxide pollutant in the atmosphere has caused considerable deterioration of the early fourteenth-century frescos by Giotto in the Scrovegni Chapel at Padua, Italy.

Not all air pollutants are eliminated by fallout, washout, or chemical reaction with surfaces. Some of the gaseous constituents have a long half-life in the atmosphere. One of them is carbon dioxide. It is harmless for health in the common concentration, but it is also an absorber of infrared radiation. Such radiation goes out from Earth's surface and is an essential element in the heat and energy balance of our planet. Carbon dioxide intercepts this radiation and thus can cause warming in the atmosphere. As an end product of all combustion processes using fossil fuels, CO_2 is gradually increasing. There is no evidence as yet that this increase has upset the energy transactions in the atmosphere, but the process requires close monitoring lest we experience a climatic change that may cause more harm than good (for crop ecology, for example). Yet we know too little to be very positive about the influence of CO_2.

We can be considerably more specific about the particulates. Aside from the effect on rainfall, it is well known that they scatter incoming solar energy. Nature has performed experiments for us by means of the ash eruptions from volcanoes. These have led to cooling and especially lowering of summer temperatures. We can be quite sure that particles from the steady effluvia of man's paravolcanic cities will have a similar effect. The masses presently involved are still small compared to the Krakatoa eruption, but the amounts are steadily climbing.

At this point it seems appropriate to consider the combined action of areas larger than a single city or metropolitan area. Weather conditions often conspire to create cumulative effects among adjacent large agglomerations of people and their activities. In many areas of the world the interurban sprawl is on the verge of fusing large metropolitan centers into the megalopolis of the future. The area from Norfolk, Virginia, to Portland, Maine, is one of them. Already there are times when the pollutant clouds of the major centers in this region overlap. If the atmospheric pressure pattern favors a weak southwest wind along this Atlantic seaboard corridor, the communities downwind not only experience fallout from pollutants of the upwind cities, but also face a continuously higher background level to which their own effluents are added. The weather conditions which may promote such cumulative clouds of pollutants either in this region or in other geographical areas are not in the once-a-century category. They are rather events that have to be expected from several times a year to once every five years. Certainly, they occur frequently enough to cause concern. These conditions also clearly show why local pollution controls are palliative but not curative. And at the present rate of expansion of population, of industry, and of automotive traffic, the time will soon be at hand when the problem will have outgrown regional and even national proportion and reach worldwide dimensions.

But even if we shrink our focus of attention to the single city we find that on a smaller scale important interactions between the built-up area and the atmosphere take place. From the viewpoint of pollution several deserve mention. Anyone who has done any flying is amazed at the murky calotte of haze over the city. It robs the inhabitants and plants of considerable illumination. In the visible region of the spectrum this loss is about 10 per cent in summer, 20 per cent in winter. It is almost impenetrable to ultraviolet wavelengths. Although there may be an argument about the benefits humans may directly derive from rays in that spectral region, their germicidal effect is unquestioned. Their lack may well account for the fact that city air has considerably higher levels of microbes than the cleaner air of the countryside.

The city also creates its own windfield. Because of its own heat production and its greater heat absorption from solar radiation it may, especially in daytime, show a larger mixing depth for pollutants than the surroundings. This is favorable to dilution if the upper winds are strong and in the right direction. There is the same beneficial effect for dispersion from high smoke stacks which discharge pollutants above the ground inversion and in the layers of accelerating winds. Yet, while the effect of lifting of pollutants either by natural or artificial means has a mitigating effect locally, it can contribute to higher concentrations (even at ground level) downstream. This is a consequence of the peculiar aerodynamic flow in the so-called planetary boundary layer. If downwind is vacant space, all is well and good, but in densely settled regions there are nearly always other communities down-wind.

These same laws of aerodynamics also introduce another effect of the city: a slow-down and diversion of air motion by ob-stacles. There is good evidence that a large city acts to some extent like a mound. Onrushing air from the outside tries to flow around rather than through it. What flows through is slowed down considerably by the roughness of the basic structural elements of the city. Wind speeds are reduced 10 to 30 per cent and, unfortunately, the largest reductions occur when the winds are weak. As is readily understood, the wind flow is particularly weakened and deflected when it hits solid blocks of buildings of uniform height. These essentially act as if a new ground surface is introduced into the air stream.

The preceding information gives some valuable hints for city planning and, especially, redevelopment. In order to maximize air flow open construction is most advantageous. Structures of variable heights are favorable, as are green spaces. Vegetation, especially shrubs and trees, acts as a filter for many pollutants if planted in sufficiently wide strips to be effective, yet not too densely to block passage of air.

Yet no plan of city redesign can offer anything but partial aid. Other measures have to go hand in hand with it. For stationary sources, as already mentioned, tall stacks help. In some instances, especially in mountainous terrain, ducting of fumes from valley locations to peaks and releasing them there has merit. In fact, such a system of smoke sewers is now actually in operation in some parts of the world. However, we are just beginning to cope with the mobile sources of pollution, the motor cars. To be sure, the government has set certain standards which will have to be met by the exhaust systems of new cars. This is a good start. Nonetheless, the number of cars is multiplying so rapidly that the total amount of effluent will not be appreciably reduced, particularly because older cars are not included and because considerable doubt attaches to the durability of the pollution-reducing devices. It is late, indeed, to design alterations for present cars to bring them to a level of personal and economic acceptability. Not that there is a lack of possibilities: electric cars, steamer cars, fuel-cell powered cars, piggy-back cars, improvement of mass transportation. Any and all of these will help, but progress has been slow and too much geared to federal initiatives.

In summary: Air pollution clearly is one of the most important elements affecting the ecology, if not the survival, of that new subspecies of man, *Homo sapiens urbanus.* This pollution has grown in direct proportion to the size of the cities. At least half of it, at present, is caused by motor vehicles. The rate of production overwhelms the natural dissipating forces of the atmosphere at increasingly frequent intervals. The problem has lost its local aspects and has to be dealt with at least on a regional basis. But many experts are fully aware that in some respect national and even worldwide concerns are involved. It has not yet been fully established to what extent pollutants interfere with global and local climates, but some effects are present beyond reasonable doubt. One can still hope that their geographical spread is limited. But who wants to gamble with drought or freezes? And who wants to introduce additional causes for sickness and death? Who wants to see further damages to natural, ornamental, and crop vegetation? Instead of answering these rhetorical questions, let us state the remedy. It involves nothing less than stopping pollution at the sources. This is the goal. Inertia, economic and technological obstacles have to be overcome. This is the task of scientist and engineer, citizen and public official. It cannot be postponed: The time is now.

REFERENCES

Bryson, R. A. 1968. All other factors being constant—a reconciliation of several theories of climatic change. *Weatherwise* 21:56–61.
Callendar, G. S. 1958. On the amount of carbon dioxide in the atmosphere. *Tellus* 10:243–248.

Chovin, P. 1967. Carbon monoxide: analysis of exhaust gas investigations in Paris. *Env. Res.* 1:198–216.

Domrös, M. 1966. *Luftverunreinigung und Stadtklima im Rheinisch-Westfälischen Industriegebiet und ihre Auswirkungen auf den Flechtenbewuchs der Bäume. Arb. z. Rhein. Landeskunde* (Bonn), Heft 23, 132 pp.

Evelyn, J. 1661. Fumifugium: or the inconvenience of the air and smoke of London dissipated. Oxford, 43 pp. (Reprinted 1933.)

Holzworth, G. C. 1967. Mixing depths, wind speeds and air pollution potential for selected locations in the United States. *Jour. Appl. Meteorol.* 6: 1039–1044.

Landsberg, H. E. 1956. The climate of towns. In *Man's role in changing the face of the earth*, ed. by William L. Thomas, Jr., University of Chicago Press, xxxviii + 1193 pp. (pp. 584–606).

Landsberg, H. E. 1966. Air pollution and urban climate. *Biometeorology (Proc. 3rd Int. Biometeorol. Congr.)* 2:648–656.

Plass, G. H. 1956. The carbon dioxide theory of climatic change. *Tellus* 8: 140–154.

Slade, D. 1967. Modeling air pollution in the Washington, D.C., to Boston megalopolis. *Science* 157:1304–1307.

Stern, A. C. 1967. The changing pattern of air pollution in the United States. *Amer. Indust. Hyg. Ass. Jour.* 28:161–165.

Thomas, M. D. 1962. Sulfur dioxide, sulfuric acid aerosol and visibility in Los Angeles. *Int. Jour. Air & Water Pollution* 6:443–454.

United States Public Health Service. 1949. Air pollution in Donora, Pennsylvania. *U.S. Public Health Serv. Bull. 306*, 173 pp.

United States Public Health Service. 1962. Symposium: Air over Cities. R. A. Taft San. Engin. Center (Cincinnati), *SEC Tech. Rep. A 62–5*, 290 pp.

United States Public Health Service. 1966. Today and tomorrow in air pollution. *U.S. Public Health Serv. Publ. No. 1555*, 28 pp.

United States Public Health Service. 1966. Air pollution, a national sample. *U.S. Public Health Serv. Publ. No. 1562*, 27 pp.

CHALLENGE FOR SURVIVAL *Commentary*
by Charles F. Luce

In preparing my commentary for this program I read in full Dr. Landsberg's paper, which I strongly recommend to each participant in this conference as an excellent piece setting forth the basis of the problems of air pollution in our metropolitan areas. Dr. Landsberg has provided the ABC's of air pollution, which are important to have. I was reminded as I read it of the advice given by a judge to a young lawyer on how to argue cases. Basically, his advice was that a lawyer should always assume that the judge knows no law at all when he presents his argument; and as the judge pointed out to the young lawyer, "You'll be amazed how often that actually is the fact." Even a sophisticated audience such as this needs to know the ABC's, and therefore the fundamentals, of air pollution, and Dr. Landsberg's paper gives them.

There are several points made in Dr. Landsberg's paper that I'd like to comment on briefly. He demonstrates conclusively that air pollution must be approached not just on a city-by-city basis, nor even on a region-by-region basis, but on a national and international basis. This is not to say that in each city we mustn't fight air pollution where it occurs, but it is to say that we should not expect success in this effort unless we approach the problem over much wider geographic areas.

His paper also raises the very important question of whether the real enemy to clean air is simply the process of combustion itself. He points out that combustion always produces carbon dioxide, and that an increasing concentration of CO_2 in the air conceivably could affect the heat balance by making Earth a warmer place. If Earth became sufficiently warm, the icecaps would melt, the levels of the ocean would rise, and we'd certainly be awash in New York. This is a very serious matter, but one that is nevertheless difficult to appraise at this time.

Dr. Landsberg's paper raises the fundamental conservation problem that all of us face who are conservationists and yet, at the same time, are trying to meet the needs of mankind for a higher standard of living in the everyday world. That is the basic contradiction we must face as we make choices between the competing demands that mankind makes upon his environment. Take this matter of reducing the total amount of combustion. It seems that technologically the best way to do this would be to produce more and more of our energy not by combustion, but by nuclear processes. Certainly, our company, Consolidated Edison, is dedicated to this proposition. By 1980, we anticipate that three-fourths of the electric energy we supply to the New York area will be produced in nuclear plants.

Nuclear energy doesn't completely eliminate pollution problems. In fact, it may cause other types of pollution. There are some low-level radioactive gases in the vicinity of nuclear power plants which, although the Atomic Energy Commission and the industry believe they are not of significance, nevertheless have concerned a number of people. There's the problem of what we do with radioactive wastes. After we burn nuclear fuel, we have a residuum that must be disposed of and is dangerous if not properly managed. Until now we have been burying it in nuclear cemeteries under conditions which require, in perpetuity, that the tanks be kept secure so that the nuclear waste won't leak out into the soil and contaminate subsurface water.

Nuclear plants present another problem: like fossil-fired plants they produce excess heat which must be dissipated into the atmosphere directly or through cooling water. Only about one-third of the energy produced in a nuclear plant is converted into electricity. The other two-thirds create a waste disposal problem. This raises questions of environmental pollution. If we dispose of the waste heat through rivers or tidal estuaries, we affect their ecology to some extent. If we do not use rivers or other natural bodies of water to dissipate the excess heat, but dissipate it directly into the air with cooling towers, we produce water vapor which, although not to be compared with sulfur dioxide, is not a pleasant thing, particularly if one lives downwind from a cooling tower.

What all this means, perhaps, is that the only way ultimately to conserve our environment in its present state is to stop all growth, especially population growth. Perhaps, instead of our belonging exclusively to such conservation groups as the Sierra Club and the Audubon Society, we should concentrate more of our efforts on the Planned Parenthood societies.

Relationship between plants and atmosphere

DAVID M. GATES

All life on this planet Earth lives in a thin shell, the biosphere, which is sandwiched between rock and sky and subjected to the warmth of vulcanism below and the irradiation of sunlight above. Man's evolution and very presence on this planet depended entirely upon plants. The atmosphere of oxygen, nitrogen, ozone, carbon dioxide, and trace gases (with its warmth, winds, and water) appeared until recently to be an inexhaustible resource available for any use or abuse. The atmosphere too, in its present form, was a consequence of plant evolution. Yet, way back in time, perhaps 600 million years ago, geological and geophysical events set the stage for life to begin within the aquatic brew of shallow seas. From then to the present, plants, animals, atmosphere, soil, and water have been dynamically interdependent. Now man changes the time scale by introducing great perturbations of the system through the exploitation of all resources. The dynamic equilibria of the past, or even the natural oscillations of the Earth ecosystem, involving land, water, atmosphere, and life, are no longer the only responses to the forces present, but new impulsive stresses are imposed by man.

What do we know of the relationships between plants and atmosphere? What does the atmosphere mean to man? How may we use our knowledge to assure sensible management of the global ecosystem? What is the capacity of the system to absorb unnatural stresses? Where do we go from here? Let us review for a moment the evolution of plants and atmosphere.

EVOLUTION OF PLANTS AND ATMOSPHERE

Not all planets have an atmosphere conducive to life, nor do all planets have a geophysical environment suitable for life to evolve. This is not to say there may not be life elsewhere in our solar system, such as on Mars or Venus, nor elsewhere in other solar systems. It is highly probable that life exists in many places in the universe.

Although the earliest organisms may have existed one billion years ago (see Barghoorn, Meinschein, and Schopf 1965), the Earth's atmosphere was very different then, and the terrestrial environment was inhospitable to any form of life. The primordial atmosphere was transparent to ultraviolet radiation from the sun, which not only irradiated the Earth's surface, but also penetrated to 5 or 10 meters depth in water. Oxygen levels in the primitive atmosphere were less than 0.001 of the present atmospheric level (P.A.L.) and originated from the photodissociation of water vapor. The rise of oxygen in the atmosphere from the primitive low levels can result only from photosynthesis, a process which will occur in large amounts only when continental extensions and climatic conditions are right. When the oxygen content of the atmosphere exceeded 0.01 P.A.L., the ocean surfaces were sufficiently screened from ionizing ultraviolet to permit abundant extension of life throughout the oceans. This oxygen level is defined by Berkner and Marshall (1963) as the "first critical level" for the explosive evolutionary advance of life during Cambrian times. With extensive photosynthesis in the oceans releasing oxygen into the atmosphere, the "second critical level" was exceeded, that is, 0.1 P.A.L., and the land surfaces became better shielded from the actinic solar ultraviolet. Now an explosive evolution of land organisms began at the end of the Silurian period, and as a result of greatly increased photosynthesis the oxygen concentration of the atmosphere rose rapidly until the Carboniferous period, when it began to approach present levels. It is possible that during the Carboniferous period the oxygen concentration reached 10 P.A.L. The oxygen concentration oscillated during Paleozoic, Mesozoic, and Cenozoic times because of the phase lag between production and consumption.

The intimate relationship between the evolution of plants and the oxygen content of the atmosphere is clear. It is well known that oxygen acts as an inhibitor in photosynthesis, even though the presence of oxygen in the atmosphere results from photosynthesis. If man's activities were to consume oxygen more rapidly than it is released by plants, the plants might grow better; but animals might not do so well. Furthermore, oxygen levels within a factor of 10 of present levels are necessary to screen out the ultraviolet rays of the sun. Oxygen in the atmosphere photodissociates and forms ozone which concentrates in the stratosphere and strongly absorbs the short ultraviolet rays of the sun.

Carbon dioxide. Plants assimilate carbon dioxide in photosynthesis. An increase in the carbon-dioxide concentration of the atmosphere by 5 to 10 times causes plants to grow luxuriantly. This leads one to believe that the present concentration of carbon dioxide is low compared with that which may have existed during plant evolution in earlier times. This is consistent with the fact that the Earth's climate was generally warmer during most of geologic time. We know that higher CO_2 concentrations cause the Earth's surface and atmosphere to be warmer because of the screening of the Earth's surface by the CO_2 against the loss of infrared radiation to space.

The concentration of carbon dioxide in the Earth's atmosphere probably has fluctuated considerably with time. Besides the atmosphere, which has 0.03 per cent carbon dioxide, the other major reservoirs are the oceans, rocks, and living organisms. The oceans contain about 50 times more carbon dioxide than the air, which contains 2.3 trillion tons. The oceans exchange about 200 billion tons of CO_2 with the atmosphere each year. When the atmospheric concentration rises, the ocean tends to absorb much of the excess; and when it falls, the ocean replenishes the atmosphere. Plants consume about 60 billion tons of CO_2 per year, but release about an equal amount through respiration. By burning fossil fuels, man dumps approximately 6 billion tons of CO_2 into the atmosphere each year. Agricultural practices release another 2 billion tons per year. Crops store much less carbon dioxide than forests do. When the atmospheric concentration rises, plants use more CO_2 for photosynthesis, but then in turn release more through respiration. Most of the CO_2 added to the atmosphere by human activities ultimately will be absorbed by the oceans. It takes about 1,000 years for the carbon-dioxide pressure of the atmosphere to come into equilibrium with the CO_2 pressure in the oceans. Hence, changes in CO_2 concentration of the atmosphere produced by man's activities which occur relatively quickly (that is, of the order of 10 to 100 years) are not corrected by oceanic uptake. During the last 100 years, man has added about 360 billion tons of CO_2 to the atmosphere through the burning of fossil fuels. According to calculations concerning the radiative "greenhouse effect," this would produce an increase of about 0.7°C in the average temperature of the globe. This is almost exactly the average increase recorded on a worldwide basis. By the year 2,000, at the present rate we will have dumped a trillion tons of CO_2 into the atmosphere and raised the mean temperature by 2.0°C. If this rate continues for 1,000 years, and we allow for the equilibrium time response of the oceans, the atmosphere will have 10 times more CO_2 than it does today and its average temperature will be 13°C warmer than today—a catastrophic situation.

Other temperature trends resulting from man's activities seem to have set in. Since 1950 there has been a steep cooling trend, and much of the warming of the first half of this century has been reversed. This is not for lack of CO_2, which is still increasing; but the cooling trend may be the result of atmospheric particulates: aerosols and the many jet contrails which are occuring throughout the world. These will increase the Earth's albedo and reduce the amount of sunlight reaching the surface.

The carbon-dioxide content of the atmosphere is on the average about 320 ppm and is increasing at the annual rate of 0.75 ppm.

Water vapor. Plants lose water by transpiration and in so doing represent an extension of the soil surface to the depths of their roots. By pulling water out of the soil at considerable depth, plants can transpire long after a bare soil would have dried out at the surface. A plant processes 200 to 900 pounds of water for every pound of dry matter produced.

A considerable amount of controversy has existed over the question of whether or not a plant canopy loses more water than a free water surface. The maximum difference cannot be great, since it depends entirely on the energy budget of the surface. If the free water surface and a vegetation surface absorb about the same amount of sunlight, then after reradiation and convection are accounted for the remainder of the energy goes to evaporation or transpiration. Whether one or the other is greater depends on the temperature of the surfaces involved. Plants do have some control over rates of water loss through the behavior of their stomates.

From energy budget considerations we can now calculate with considerable accuracy the water loss from any plant for any given environmental conditions. This gives us a great deal of insight to the dynamics of water loss from a leaf surface.

Atmospheric aerosols. There remains considerable speculation concerning the degree to which bluish hazes in the atmosphere are contributed to by volatile organic substances from plants, mainly terpene-like hydrocarbons. There is little doubt that organic substances are released by plants into the atmosphere. The unanswered questions have to do with the rate at which they go from plants to air, their specific identity, and the role they play in the atmosphere. Do these photo-organic substances actually end up as Aitken nuclei to form blue hazes?

Went (1960) has estimated that approximately 1.7×10^8 tons of volatile organic materials are released from plants into the air each year. It has been said that plants pollute the atmosphere. It is my opinion that this is not true. Whatever substances plants do contribute to the atmosphere are part of the natural features of the landscape and cannot be classified as pollutants. Only the products of man's activities may be considered as pollutants.

Wind. A major role in the exchange of gases among soil, plants, and atmosphere is played by wind. At the same time, plants have a major influence on the flow of wind over the Earth's surface. The climate of regions without plants, such as deserts, is windy and gusty. The drag force produced by plants projecting into the air is extremely important, and without it the loose surface of our planet would be blown about much of the time. A surface without plants becomes dry, and the incident solar radiation is dissipated by reradiation and by strong convective motion of the air. A dry wind-swept surface puts dust into the air and the dust attenuates the solar radiation. The dust may produce more radiative cooling of the air aloft, causing it to sink towards the surface. As it sinks, it warms adiabatically and retains moisture, thereby not allowing precipitation. This aggravates the drought at the surface, and desert conditions are enhanced. This actually appears to be the cause of the Rajputana desert of northwestern India, according to Bryson (1967).

All surfaces, including our own, have air adhering to them in what is referred to as a boundary layer. This boundary layer can be seen at times, and it can be photographed. It can be experienced when one takes a bath in warm water. Immediately after getting into the water, it seems to us that it has cooled significantly. There has been very little cooling, but the boundary layer of water next to our skin has been established and the water next to the skin is at the skin temperature, but the water a few millimeters or more beyond our surface is still nearly as warm as when we stepped into it. When I take a sauna bath (I once took one at 230°F), the boundary layer of air next to my surface partially insulates me against the intense heat. Plant leaves possess boundary layers which impede the flow of water vapor, carbon dioxide, oxygen, and other gases between the leaf and the air. When the wind blows, it wipes away the boundary layer and enhances gas exchange. The very slightest breeze, less than 1 mph speed, significantly reduces the thickness of the boundary layer. Usually an increase in wind will produce an increase in moisture loss from a leaf, but it may also produce a decrease in transpiration. The really significant wind speeds in the vicinity of any single leaf are the low wind speeds, less than 3 mph. However, when plant canopies as a whole are considered, conditions of strong winds above the canopy become significant within the canopy. Certainly high winds aloft are necessary in order to get some air movement within canopies or near the ground.

The air inside a forest or inside a dense crop is relatively still compared to the air movement above the stand. Local heating of vegetation and soil by sunlight always causes some air movement. When the wind blows strong above a stand of vegetation, there is great attenuation of the wind as the top of the stand is approached and much further attenuation as one goes into the stand itself. Beyond the edge of the forest or in the field beyond the hedge row, the wind is reduced to a distance of nearly 30 times the height of the barrier. The shelterbelts of the plains of Kansas were planted to reduce the impact of the wind on the fields. A barrier of trees produces a "snow fence" effect. It causes snow to accumulate heavily in the field just beyond the line of trees. The Canterbury plain of New Zealand, which is swept by strong catabic winds, is planted with great rows of pines (*Pinus radiata*) in order to increase the drag effects on the winds and slow the air movement.

The turbulent air flow across the vegetated forests and plains is exceedingly important as a mixing process which renews the air—cleansing the air of pollutants, renewing the oxygen and carbon dioxide of the air, and humidifying it as well.

Temperature. A surface without plants in the hot summer sun is very hot indeed. Bare soil surface temperatures can reach 160°F in the hot summer sun. A person on the surface must contend not only with the high air temperature but also with the enormous reflected radiation in addition to the direct radiation. Urban environments often are nearly this warm, and the heat load placed on buildings requires enormous expenditures for air conditioning. Plants cool the air around them by transpiration. If the hot summer winds traverse hundreds of miles of bare soil or pavement instead of grass, shrubs, or trees, then the air becomes hotter by the mile. The shade leaves of plants in the daytime are usually 2° to 5°F cooler than the air near them, and the tops of canopies are colder than the air at night because they radiate to the cold night sky. On the other hand, bare soil heats up all day and retains the heat at night. When a hot wind out of the southwest blasts us with the heat of summer, it is certain that this hot wind would be 5° to 10°F warmer if it had traversed pavement or soil rather than vegetation.

Our major cities are monstrous heat islands and dust domes. They have 10 per cent more cloudiness, 10 per cent more precipitation, 25 per cent less wind, and 30 per cent more fog in summer and 100 per cent more in winter. The mean annual temperature within a city is 10° to 15°F warmer than in the country.

THE FUTURE

What does it all mean when man paves nearly 1 per cent of the United States with roads and highways; when he shifts the landscape from the diversity of natural communities to plant monocultures; when he sends into the atmosphere billions of tons of dust a year; when he changes the climate of vast areas occupied by cities; when he uses the streams, lakes, oceans, and atmosphere as a giant garbage dump? Today our abuse of the landscape is catching up with us at a rate which is exceeding our ability to understand and deal with the complexity of the situation. Where do we go from here?

Basic research concerning the interaction of the atmosphere with the vegetation surface is desperately needed. We do not understand the detailed interaction of the plants with the atmosphere. We know that plants must take out of the air some of the pollutants generated in the industrial areas, for plants are severely damaged by the photochemical products of pollution. In order for a plant to assimilate, it must take in CO_2 through its stomates and in doing so will also take in all other gases. One can only surmise that contaminated air from a manufacturing plant is partially cleansed if it flows through a dense vegetation canopy rather than if it comes directly across concrete paving to its victims. The trees and shrubs of a city must aid materially in filtering the dust from the air as it settles out on their surfaces.

What do we do about this and where do we go from here? Honestly, I do not know, except that I am sure of one thing. We need to marshall a crash program of national urgency to understand the dynamics of the surface of our landscape. We have an important branch of chemistry known as surface chemistry and a branch of physics known as surface physics. We now need to concentrate our attention on surface botany, surface meteorology, and surface geophysics—perhaps to be called *surface ecology*. If science does not soon become capable of understanding the dynamics of the surface on which we live and upon which we depend for survival, then all the machinery, weapons, chemicals, and molecular biology will come to naught. Never has anyone really worked to establish the true dynamics, thermodynamics, and gas exchange of the living surface of this Earth. Nor have we made a detailed study of these subjects pertaining to the surfaces of urban areas. We need to launch operations-research types of studies concerning the detailed dynamics of landscapes and urban surfaces. If a Rand Corporation was needed to estimate the optimum strategies of warfare, it is every bit as essential that we estimate the optimum strategies of urban development.

I should like to close my remarks with the statement I made to the Daddario Hearings before the Subcommittee on Science, Research, and Development of the Committee on Science and Astronautics of the United States House of Representatives, 3 August 1967. I said that if we do not take drastic action soon,

"We will go down in history as an elegant technological society struck down by biological disintegration for lack of ecological understanding."

REFERENCES

Barghoorn, E. S., W. G. Meinschein, and J. W. Schopf. 1965. Paleobiology of a precambrian shale. *Science* 148:461–472.

Berkner, L. V., and L. C. Marshall. 1963. On the growth of oxygen in the Earth's atmosphere. Manuscript, private communication.

Bryson, R. A. 1967. Is man changing the climate of the Earth. *Saturday Review of Literature*, 1 April, pp. 52–55.

Went, F. W. 1960. Organic matter in the atmosphere, and its possible relation to petroleum formation. *Proc. Natl. Acad. Sci.* (U.S.) 46: 212–221.

CHALLENGE FOR SURVIVAL *Commentary*
by Carl Thompson

I noted that Dr. Pierre Dansereau's paper refers to the need for science writers "versed in Madison Avenue techniques." Not being exposed to that Avenue's environmental influences, for better or for worse, I am not quite certain what is implied by "Madison Avenue techniques." I assume it refers to some kind of communication, which is our business. I should confess, perhaps with shame rather than pride, that when we established our Environmental Health Unit between Third and Lexington Avenues, I suggested we were in the wrong location; that because we were dealing with words and matters of health, we probably should locate about half-way between "Lexicon" and "Medicine" avenues.

Communication is one of the most pervasive and persuasive of modern environmental factors. Too often it can be, like other factors, a pollutant. But communication need not be a pollutant and, indeed, must not be, if society is to cope intelligently, effectively, and acceptably with other compelling problems of the environment.

Dr. Gates posed the question: Will man always be susceptible to inadvertent change and consequence? Given the nature of man (as man and beast) the answer has to be yes. And one reason is that, as a communicating animal, man is always susceptible to bad as well as good communication—and even to lack of communication.

To us, communication does not mean just mass publicity or "Madison Avenue techniques." Communication means Dr. Gates's serving on a National Committee for Air Quality Criteria with business, government leaders, and fellow scientists, as he is doing. Communication means the hearings conducted by Representative Daddario of Connecticut and referred to by Dr. Gates, which are continuing dialogues between a legislative group and representatives of science, industry, and government.

Many environmental health problems stem from lack of good

communications; they call for better public understanding and fresh public policies. In our Environmental Health Unit, we operate and counsel on several basic assumptions. Some of these are:

that our society is doing many, many things to our environment without really knowing what the outcome will be.

that industry has a selfish interest as well as a public responsibility to help study, analyze, understand, control, and prevent problems created by insults to the environment.

that the public has a right to be accurately informed about the vast complexities of environmental problems, about what industry and government are doing about these problems, and about the public's own role in both creating and solving the problems.

that the public will increasingly support steps, whether by industry or government, to achieve improvement in environmental quality as rapidly as is feasible, and

that companies and industries must get deeply involved. They must assign responsibility for developing knowledge, policies, and practices for environmental control programs at high management level, similar to those applied to other aspects of business.

In the past few years, much progress has been made by many companies and entire industries in assuming responsibilities and initiating practices in the area of environmental control. Of course, more needs to be done, and industry is doing more. Just this morning I saw an article in *International Industrial Medicine and Surgery*, describing the environmental control program within Johns-Manville Corporation. Procter and Gamble has a similar, total-environment approach. Many oil and steel companies, for example, are adopting top-level programs for environmental control.

If some are a little late in doing so, or are not moving as fast as you think they should, it is because, in part through lack of good communication, top managements have not realized how important a part they can and must play if environmental control programs are going to work.

All those concerned with environmental health problems could well re-examine their responsibilities in communicating with the various publics. This is an important problem for the scientists. If industry has been slow to learn how to work with and listen to scientists, it is also true that some scientists are slow to learn how to work with industry and other important segments of the public. Here again is a communications problem. There is increasing need for translating scientific jargon into accurate and intelligible English, not into another jargon such as sensational journalism. Scientists may mean what they say, but they don't always say what they mean.

Professional writers and communicators can help scientists say what they mean. Although there is always danger of oversimplification, sometimes this may be better than over-obfuscation. There is need today for better analyses of scientific reports and data and interpretation of what they do or do not mean, so that proper decisions for action can be taken.

Communication also means developing information that is understandable to the public. For example, watching what issues from Consolidated Edison's stacks, many people comment on "what they're doing to the skies." In that few minutes, fifty cars and four buses go by, and cigarettes are tossed into the street. And still they say, "Look what Con Edison is doing to us." Dr. Landsberg's slides show that transportation contributes to air pollution some four times more than does electric power generation. I think people generally don't understand that when they flick on their electric light, turn on their dishwasher, run out to the automobile and dash down to the store to buy a pack of cigarettes, they are contributing with each of those actions to the problems that we are trying to solve.

In communicating about scientific studies, writers and scientists could well take more caution in differentiating between the sensational suspect and the established hazard. When I open my news clipping files and look at the headlines, I find that I am about to contract cancer or heart disease because I drink milk, I drink beer, I drink coffee, I drink tea, I drink alcohol, I drink soft water, I drink hard water. All of these have been in the headlines. I eat charcoal-broiled steak, I eat smoked fish, I eat citrus fruits, I eat honey from bees who suck at azalea blossoms. All have been reported as possible contributors to my ill health. I smoke tobacco, and I breathe city air. I play golf in the wind and the sun—cancer-causing agents. I work too hard at my job, and I don't work hard enough at my exercise. If I drive a car through the city and breathe exhaust fumes, it's very bad. But if I go for a walk in the country, I breathe the hydrocarbonaceous terpines exuded from the coniferous forests, and this too is bad.

And then I find out, on top of all this, that I probably picked the wrong parents!

I think there's no wonder incredulity is found sometimes among the informed as well as the uninformed public, when a scientist warns that a particular product or a particular activity may be killing people—who are living longer than ever. The public may not understand sophisticated science but most know about the Aesopian cry of wolf.

Last week the *Wall Street Journal* in its most popular and perhaps least controversial feature, "PEPPER . . . and Salt" (I suppose there is controversy, really, over effects of pepper and salt but the *Journal* dispenses it in small doses to add flavor to its editorial page), printed a cartoon of a bewildered gentleman scanning a newspaper and commenting to his rather forbearing wife: "I can't understand it. There's been only bad news for the last 50 years and yet we're still here."

I hope there'll be more and more good news, and good communication, about environmental quality in the next few years so that after another fifty years, people can say, "We're still here."

Radioactivity and fallout: the model pollution

GEORGE M. WOODWELL

Ecologists are so thoroughly accustomed to playing Cassandra, predicting doom, that we hardly give credit for even major postponements of the day of doom. Doom has so many components these days that it is difficult to sort out which one is more important at any moment: the crisis of the dollar, the war, the cities, the pollution, the population, or the fact that the students are going to pot. What is encouraging and central to a symposium entitled "Challenge for Survival" is the fact that there is now a broad and growing consensus that accepts the simple truth that the size of the human population is a key and that the ultimate amelioration of these crises depends on establishing some sort of equilibrium between population and resources. Establishing any such equilibrium is difficult, almost hopelessly so, not only because of the difficulties of controlling the numbers of people, but also because a burgeoning and, in some ways, malignant technology both increases certain types of resources and simultaneously destroys other essential ones. Thus an expanding technology offers ever cheaper power and transportation but also

Research carried out at Brookhaven National Laboratory under the auspices of the U.S. Atomic Energy Commission. Reprinted from *Garden Journal* (18)4: 100–104, 1968; lightly edited.

threatens to degrade the environment in diverse ways, one of the most important being with wastes that are biologically active.

RADIATION POLLUTION

My objective is to summarize the broader scientific aspects of the problems associated with release of certain types of toxic wastes into the environment. Atomic energy provides a model, unfinished, rough-hewn in many of its parts, polished in others, but overall a brilliant example of the marshalling of scientific and political talent on an international scale to mitigate a worldwide pollution problem. That problem has not been solved, but there's hope that it can be and there are many lessons to be learned from it. I propose to examine the radiation-pollution problem and to show how it can be used to contribute to a solution of certain other analogous pollution problems, especially those we have now with pesticides, which appear to be the world's most dangerous pollutants.

Assumption of dilution and the right to pollute. The attitudes that allowed worldwide contamination of the Earth with radio-activity and which now allow other even more serious pollutions are important and still dominant, although weakening. The most important assumption that led to the problems with radioactivity is the assumption of dilution. Toxic materials released into the environment are widely assumed to be diluted to innocuousness. If there are local effects from the toxicity, they are transient; an abundant and vigorous nature repairs any damage within at most a few years—or the effects are accepted as small cost for technological progress. The assumption is practical and as long as the environment is very large in comparison with the quantity of the release, "dilution" appears to occur. At least the material "disappears."

So thoroughly ingrained is this philosophy that its corollary, the right to pollute, has become a second major philosophical and, for somewhat different reasons, legal assumption: we tend to require detailed scientific proof of direct, personal damage to man as a prerequisite for even considering restriction of any right to pollute.

On the basis of these two suppositions, dilution and the assumption of the right to pollute until proof of damage, we, man, all over the world, are now well embarked on a program of releasing unmeasured quantities of quite literally thousands of different kinds of biologically active substances into the general environment. It is one of the spectacular contradictions of our time that in the age of science we should be entering blindly on a thousand unplanned, uncontrolled, unmonitored, unguided, largely unrestrained, and totally unscientific experiments with the whole world as the subject and with survival at hazard.

Assumption of dilution is a trap. The assumption of dilution, so easy to make, so cheap, so comforting, so much a part of human nature, is a trap. Biologically active materials released into the biosphere travel in patterns that are surprisingly well known. A major contribution of atomic energy has been definition of these patterns, using as tracers the radioactivity in fallout from bomb tests. Intensive studies began in earnest only after the series of bomb tests known as "Castle" were set off in the Pacific in the spring of 1954. This was the series, some of you will recall, that included the test that dropped fallout on Rongelap Atoll, exposing its inhabitants, numbering about 65, to an estimated 175 R (500 R is widely accepted as the mean lethal exposure for man). A Japanese fishing vessel, the Lucky Dragon, and its crew were also caught in the fallout; and for several months tuna caught in the Pacific and landed in Japan were sufficiently radioactive that authorities would not allow them to be sold. In the eyes of the world this series of misfortunes was "proof of damage" and frightening proof of a new-found capacity to degrade the environment in places far removed from those affected directly by the blast and the ionizing radiation accompanying the bomb. Some of the radioactivity from these tests is of course still circulating through the biosphere. It was this series of frightening events that triggered sufficient public interest in the problems of worldwide pollution with radioactivity to mount a really significant international research program tracing these patterns (UNSCEAR 1958, 1962, 1964) and that ultimately resulted in the treaty among the more civilized nations banning nuclear tests in the atmosphere.

Research on man-made radioactivity. From the research on man-made radioactivity we have learned these things, all relevant and even basic to the greater problems of pollution that we are just now beginning to recognize as a major "challenge to survival."

First, particulate matter, introduced into the lower atmosphere, enters air currents that move around the world in periods of fifteen to twenty-five days in the middle latitudes, sometimes less.

Second, the half-time of residence (time for one-half the material to be removed) of particulate matter carried in these currents ranges between a few days and a month, the same general range as the time to travel around the world. Thus it is no surprise these days to measure the radioactive cloud produced by tests in central Asia on several successive trips around the world.

Third, such material tends to be removed from the air and deposited on the ground by precipitation, more in the early precipitation of any storm than later.

Fourth, the patterns apply to any particulate matter entering the air currents of the troposphere. Some fraction of the pollen, for instance, that is released by plants close to the ground surface enters these patterns and is transported in air and deposited in precipitation (Gatz and Dingle 1965).

Movement of radionuclides through living systems. Hardly less important, we know that certain radionuclides are accumulated from the environment into the tissues of plants and animals, where they may be concentrated in high degree, concentration factors of 100- to 1000-fold and higher being common. But the patterns of movement of radionuclides through ecological systems are not capable of simple generalization: each radionuclide travels its own peculiar path. Thus Cs^{137} behaves in ways that are similar to K and tends to be accumulated in muscle, with the greatest amounts in older organisms and in carnivores. The accumulation of Cs^{137} in Eskimos through the lichen-caribou food chain is well known. Sr^{90}, however, is accumulated in bones and herbivores get most of it; I^{131}, in thyroids; Fe^{55}, in blood and elsewhere. Discovery of these patterns has required intensive research on each substance, both to trace its movement through the patterns of air and water circulation and to discover its pathways through living systems (Polikarpov 1966; Åberg and Hungate 1967).

The hazard of ionizing radiation. But this is only part of the story. It documents the fact that dilution into an infinite environment is not a safe assumption. And what of the effects? Again the story is not a simple one, each substance presenting its own peculiar set of hazards. With ionizing radiation the problem seems reasonably straightforward, although not always so to those charged with developing standards of safety. There is general agreement that the principal danger is a direct hazard to man through damage to the genetic material, "mutations," which are, for the practical purposes of this discussion, all deleterious. Man is most vulnerable because radiation causes an increase in the frequency of deleterious mutations, in the jargon, an increase in the "genetic load," by adding to the numbers of genetically-determined unfortunates. If man is protected from this hazard, levels of man-made radiation in nature will almost certainly be so low as to have no significant effects on other organisms, because in these species, unlike man, genetic unfortunates are removed by selection. Increasing mutation rates will probably not increase rates of evolution as so often assumed. Thus the risk from ionizing radiation, released from whatever source, is first a direct hazard to man; this is not so for many other toxic substances as we shall see in a moment.

How much radiation is "safe"? But again, there is no simple answer to the question of how much radiation is "safe." It would be very convenient if there were some threshold below which ionizing radiation has no effect. A considerable weight of evidence suggests that there is no threshold for production of mutations; even very low exposures increase mutation frequencies slightly. On the other hand, there is clear benefit from radiation exposures in medicine, but it is not possible to enjoy the benefits of nuclear power without some small increase in radiation exposure for workers in the plant. Thus we must arrive at a compromise in exposing people directly, limiting direct exposures around nuclear plants systematically and vigorously to those well below levels that increase genetic hazards appreciably.

Cycling of radioactive wastes is a worldwide problem. But the problems raised by the cycling of radioactive wastes are different. It is more difficult to anticipate exposure, more difficult to make even a reasonable guess as to how much of any nuclide will appear in human tissues. And, because of the movement of air and water around the world, the problem for long-lived materials suddenly becomes not merely a local one, confined to the Hudson River Estuary, the Columbia River, the Irish Sea, or the Bay of Biscay, all water bodies now receiving appreciable radioactive wastes, but a universal one. Each increment of waste enters a worldwide pool of that material. Once we recognize that many pollution problems are world problems, not local ones, then we can approach them systematically, estimating the totals that we are willing to have in the biosphere at one time.

Radioactive materials decay at some constant rate, often defined as "half-life," the time for half the activity to be lost. Thus there is a constant rate of removal of any radioactive substance from the environment due simply to physical decay. If we know that a quantity (A) of a substance is released into the environment regularly and that at the end of time (t) the fraction $\frac{A_t}{A_o} = R$ remains, then the amount (S) present after n units of time will be:

$$S = A \frac{(1 - R^n)}{1 - R} \tag{1}$$

R is related to half-life $(t_{1/2})$ by:

$$R = e^{-0.693 \frac{t}{t_{1/2}}} \tag{2}$$

where t is the period for which the retention rate is derived and t and $t_{1/2}$ are in the same units. The equilibrium concentration will be given by assuming that $n \to \infty$, when

$$S = \frac{A}{1 - R} \tag{3}$$

Thus the equilibrium concentration of something with a half-life in the range of one year will be about twice the annual release. If the half-life is ten years, the equilibrium will be about fifteen times the annual release. A material with a half-life of thirty years, such as Cs^{137}, will achieve an equilibrium in the environment that is about fifty times the annual release. If the substance is sequestered in forms that make it unavailable for circulation through living systems, then the equilibrium calculated on the basis of physical half-life will simply state the maximum that could be circulating. The actual amount will depend on the efficiency of the mechanism that sequesters the radioactivity. Cs^{137}, for example, circulates freely in biological systems, but tends to be fixed in certain micaceous clays and thereby effectively removed from further circulation. The rate of fixation in clays, however, is not easily estimated.

What is clear is that there is need to relate the input of toxic wastes to their worldwide equilibria and these equilibria to the changes such concentrations will induce in the biosphere. With ionizing radiation man is more vulnerable than his environment. The most serious radiation hazards will ultimately arise from gases such as tritium and Kr^{85} which are long-lived, produced in appreciable quantities, and very difficult to contain. The problems may be aggravated as atomic energy becomes more widely used by industry, because the interests of long-term safety and industrial profits are not always coincident. And there will be other proposals such as the one to build a new Isthmian canal with nuclear explosives. There is much more evidence, however, to suggest that we know how to control these problems than there is that we recognize and can control other analogous ones.

THE PERSISTENT PESTICIDES

There are probably large quantities of many different kinds of metabolites of civilization circulating in the biosphere right now, substances that are released in large quantities, are biologically active, have long half-lives, and therefore present problems that are analogous to those presented by ionizing radiation. The persistent pesticides, however, seem to cause by far the greatest problem, but not, strangely enough, by poisoning man. With pesticides there is, of course, a hazard to man, but we have taken pains to insulate man's food chain by elaborate regulations. By and large these regulations are effective, although not always (The New York Times). What has happened is that we have at least temporarily protected man but we have allowed virtually unlimited uses of long-lived pesticides in any place that will not contaminate human food produced in agriculture. The result has been the accumulation in the biosphere of concentrations of persistent pesticides, especially DDT, that are quite clearly degrading ecological systems all over the world. The extent of the changes is far from clear. What is evident is that certain carnivorous and scavenging birds the world over are suffering rapid reductions in reproductive capacity that seem clearly related to pesticide burdens. This applies even to oceanic birds, such as the Bermuda petrel, that do not come into contact with man or with sprayed areas (Wurster and Wingate 1968). But there is ample reason to believe that many groups in addition to birds are affected, including oceanic fishes and perhaps even phytoplankton, the basis of all oceanic food chains (Wurster 1968). The trend, if allowed to continue, will follow the familar pattern set by eutrophication of Lake Erie and numerous other smaller lakes, now being followed rapidly by Lake Michigan.

Although we may be able to afford to lose lakes in this way, we cannot afford to lose the oceans.

DDT. It is hardly surprising that we have an acute problem with pesticides when one recognizes that probably very close to 100 per cent of the world production of DDT is distributed in places where it can move freely through the various cycles of the biosphere. There is good evidence to support the assumption that the chemical degradation of pesticides follows the same pattern as radioactive decay: the amount decaying is proportional to the concentration (Hamaker 1966). This means that we can use the same arithmetic to estimate the total quantity that will be circulating in the biosphere at equilibrium if we know the half-life and the rate of release.

The half-life of pesticides in nature is not easily estimated. Studies of agricultural soils indicated a half-time for disappearance of residues of DDT in the range of two to four years. But this undoubtedly reflects several types of losses, including erosion, vaporization, co-distillation with water, and leaching into the water table as well as chemical degradation. When organic soils are present, residues tend to remain for many years (Woodwell and Martin 1964, and others). An estimate of half-life of ten years for DDT residues in biological systems seems minimum; their persistence may be considerably longer.

The annual production of pesticides in the world appears not to be tabulated. The United States Tariff Commission reports United States production of DDT. Between 1957 and 1967 production ranged between 99,000,000 and 179,000,000 pounds, with the highest in 1963. In 1967 production was about 103 million pounds. The mean for the eleven-year period was about 147 million pounds. If United States production is 75 per cent of world production, then we might assume with some justification that the world equilibrium would be based on an annual release of 200 million pounds into the biosphere. The total amount of DDT residues circulating in the biosphere would then be about 3 billion pounds, but this equilibrium would be approached only after 75 years. If we had used DDT at this high rate since 1946 we would now have about 1.5 billion pounds in the biosphere or about one-half the total we would have if the residues came to equilibrium under these conditions. Thus we can expect far greater changes in the world's biota than we've seen so far if we continue using these long-lived pesticides at the rate we have used them in the past decade.

My colleagues will be quick to point out that DDT production in the United States has dropped in the past year, and there is some evidence of a downward trend in a period when total use of pesticides is increasing abruptly. With more than a billion pounds of DDT now cycling in the biosphere, and with abundant evidence of effects, there can hardly be a downward trend in use that is steep enough to avoid irreparable changes in the Earth's biota, changes that can only be deleterious to our long-term interests in survival.

SURVIVAL DEMANDS LIMITATIONS ON TECHNOLOGY

These observations simply point once more to the fact that the world is now small and we must tidy it up if we intend to continue using it very long. The history of ionizing radiation is an example of a pollution whose hazards we have appraised and whose source we have controlled. Pesticides are an example of the opposite: failure to appraise the hazards. And now there is so much political and industrial power supporting the status quo that we may not be able to control it before we have lost an important fraction of the Earth's biota, driving the whole Earth a significant step down the path that Lake Erie has followed.

To return to my original point, survival demands control of population, but it also demands some much more stringent and unpopular limitations on technology. It is true that there is some ultimate limit on the amount of power that can be produced by atomic energy without exposing man to unacceptable levels of radioactivity. It is also true that there is a limit on the amount of persistent pesticides we can tolerate circulating through the biosphere. Testing these limits as we are doing at the moment is a strange and dangerous game, suggesting that we have not yet learned that the Challenge is for Survival.

REFERENCES

Åberg, B., and F. P. Hungate (eds.). 1967. Radioecological concentration processes. *Proc. Int. Symp.*, Stockholm, April 25–29, 1966, London, Pergamon Press, 1040 pp.

Gatz, D. F., and A. N. Dingle. 1965. Air cleansing by convective storms. In *Radioactive fallout from nuclear weapons tests*, ed. by A. W. Klement, Jr., Div. Technical Information, Oak Ridge National Laboratory, Tenn., pp. 566–581.

Hamaker, J. W. 1966. Mathematical prediction of cumulative levels of pesticides in soil. In *Organic pesticides in the environment*, ed. by R. F. Gould, Advances in Chemistry Series No. 60, Washington, D.C., American Chemical Society, pp. 122–145.

New York Times. Sunday, April 7, 1968. Montana Dairies Shut in Poisoning.

Polikarpov, G. G. 1966. *Radioecology of aquatic organisms*. Translated from the Russian by Scriptu Technica, Ltd.; English translation ed. by V. Schultz and A. W. Klement, Jr., New York, Reinhold Publishing Corp., 314 pp.

Report of the United Nations Scientific Committee on the Effects of Atomic Radiation. 1958. General Assembly, Official Records: 13th Session, Suppl. No. 17.

Report of the United Nations Scientific Committee on the Effects of Atomic Radiation. 1962. General Assembly, Official Records: 17th Session, Suppl. No. 16.

Report of the United Nations Scientific Committee on the Effects of Atomic Radiation. 1964. General Assembly, Official Records: 19th Session, Suppl. No. 14.

Woodwell, G. M., and F. T. Martin. 1964. Persistence of DDT in soils of heavily sprayed forest stands. *Science* 145: 481–483.

Wurster, C. F. 1968. DDT reduces photosynthesis by marine phytoplankton. *Science* 159: 1474–1475.

Wurster, C. F., and D. B. Wingate. 1968. DDT residues and declining reproduction in the Bermuda petrel. *Science* 159: 979–981.

CHALLENGE FOR SURVIVAL *Commentary*

by Mathew M. Shapiro

I agree, except in small part, with what **Dr. Woodwell** had to say. I am a physical scientist. I am responsible for laboratories where uranium, plutonium, and other radioactive materials are used, and I feel most comfortable in commenting on that part of his paper that deals with radioactivity.

The problem, as I see it, is that society has not developed a reasonable set of guidelines for determining acceptability in the balance that we have to make between benefits and hazards. This we must do. The very first step is to learn how to assign quantitative values to the benefits and quantitative values to the hazards. Dr. Woodwell in his published work has done this, and I think you got a feeling from some of the other speakers that they, too, were trying to become quantitative. We find no difficulty in deciding that the benefit of penicillin to millions of people outweighs the hazards to a few who are allergic to it. We find no difficulty in deciding that the deleterious effects of thalidomide on children outweigh the benefits of increased fertility that the drug bestows. But all the cases are not so easy to decide.

Consider the example of lead. Lead is ubiquitous. It occurs in food and water, in the home, and in industry. It is suspected of being a causative factor in diseases such as cancer, multiple sclerosis, and vascular disorders. It is believed to shorten man's lifetime. More than forty years ago the Surgeon General convened a panel of distinguished experts which almost doomed the use of tetraethyl lead in gasoline. But as we know, the blow to our standard of living did not take place, and lead has been used in gasoline. A few years ago, the Surgeon General convened another panel, because a request had been made to increase the amount of lead in gasoline. *There were still no clear guidelines for the experts on this panel to use, after forty years of consideration of this problem.*

Dr. Woodwell has pointed out that the atomic energy industry provides a better model for us to follow, and at least as far as the postwar period is concerned, I agree with him. I suggest that this is due to two things. One is the quantitative approach adopted and the second is an unusual attitude that has developed in that particular industry. Extensive experiments were carried out to determine quantitatively the effects of radiation on human beings. Scientific studies were made of how radioactive sources spread both locally and throughout the world. Dr. Woodwell described this in his lecture, and there is no point in my repeating it. Suffice it to say that the Federal Radiation Protection Council formulates guidelines that establish permissible concentrations of radioactive materials in man, as well as in the air and in the water which he uses.

But that is really only half the story. The attitude toward radiation has been from the beginning, or at least since the war, that it is a hazardous substance and that the user has to prove his right to use it. This is an unusual attitude, which arises, I think, because the public was first introduced to atomic energy through the atomic bomb, a death-dealing mechanism. For whatever reason, the attitude has been defensive; it has been to expose individuals to the least possible amount of radiation, rather than to operate right up to the legal limit. For example, a study of operating reactors over a four-year period shows that the average release of radioactivity to the atmosphere was only one seven-hundredth of that which was permitted by regulation. The maximum release of any single power plant during that same period was only one three-hundredth of that which is permitted by regulation. By contrast, oil- and coal-fired plants operate at about one-tenth or so of the level which is believed to be harmful. In 1,000 reactor-years of operation—that is, the number of reactors multiplied by the number of years they have been operating—there have been only six deaths in this industry.

Up to this point, I have not disagreed with the other speakers or Dr. Woodwell; however, I think we now part company for a brief moment. One speaker suggested that, as the responsibility for handling these toxic substances is turned over to industry, there arises a conflict between the profit motive of industry and the health and safety considerations of the general population.

I dispute this. The DuPont Company is a very safety-conscious organization. They have made studies of their own operations which convince them, and which convinced me many years ago, that it is good business practice to be safe. Safety pays off in dollars and cents. It is expensive to have accidents. When you consider the cost of interrupting the functioning of an industrial plant, the medical expenses, and the legal costs, it is less expensive to sponsor safety programs and avoid accidents than it is to pay the consequences.

However—and here we come back together again—I want to point out that the availability of property-damage insurance and liability insurance is making it more difficult for the director of health and safety in a corporation to justify, on an economic basis, that his company operate in a safe fashion. This is now a big business. Property-damage premiums and liability premiums run to $20 billion per year, or 3 per cent of the Gross National Product. By paying a modest premium, the company can insure itself against property loss, against interruption of business (including loss of profits and continuing expenses while the plant is out of operation), and against third party liability. This makes the job of the safety officer much more difficult.

Consequently, the important question is one of attitude. Survival is going to depend on the attitude of individuals toward polluting the world. Our success will depend more on stimulating a negative attitude toward pollution than on the amount of economic pressure or federal regulations that we can bring to bear. In the atomic energy industry, many of us, as individuals, have adopted the viewpoint that we want to be convinced that what we are doing and the way we are doing it is safe, and then we look to the state and federal regulations and see if, incidentally, we also satisfy these. And I think this attitude has to be much more widespread if we are going to succeed.

Photo by Arthur Glowka: Spuyten Duyvil, where the
East River enters the Hudson at the boundary
of Manhattan and the Bronx, New York.

WATER

Educational, recreational, and scientific aspects of the aquatic community

DIXY LEE RAY

When we consider this ambitious topic, we cannot escape the conclusion that a proper development of any of the three aspects mentioned in the title would take us far beyond the time limits necessarily set for this discussion. For this reason I prefer to concentrate on the "aquatic environment" or "aquatic community" and ask what it is that all waters have in common? The answer of course is water itself.

Water is this Earth's most characteristic and most cherished commodity. Water is so common, so necessary, so always-present, so wholly commonplace that we often fail to see it for the remarkable material that it is. Water is unique. Water is an odd liquid; in fact, it is odd that water is liquid at all! Water has novel properties. It is these that make Earth's life possible. Without water there would be no trees, no greenbelts, no gardens, no flowers, no birdsong, no seasons, no climate, no conservation —no life at all. And no symposium. Water exists on Earth. Not on Venus, or Mars, or Mercury, or Jupiter, or Saturn—or on

Reprinted from *Garden Journal* 18(6): 169–173, 1968; lightly edited.

any of the other planets in our solar system. Earth is unique because it has water. No other planet (in our solar system—and
other solar systems don't count, they are much too far away)
can make that claim. It is time for us to stop flirting with science
fiction about other planets and face the fact that Earth alone has
water; Earth is unique; life is unique; we are unique.

Water is a funny material: a single chemical compound that
results from the binding of two hydrogen molecules with one of
oxygen—the familiar H_2O. But this material is liquid at "ordinary" temperatures from $0°$ to $100°C$ ($32°$ to $212°F$). Since we
are so accustomed to this single fact it does not seem strange to us
until we compare H_2O with other simple compounds of hydrogen. Consider nitrogen, the next lightest element to oxygen:
it combines with hydrogen to form ammonia, NH_3, a *gas* at
ordinary temperatures, and great energy is required to liquify it.
Or take fluorine, the next heaviest element to oxygen: it combines
with hydrogen to form hydrofluoric acid that is liquid only up to
$20°C$ (a cool room temperature), then goes into the gaseous
phase at all high temperatures. Or carbon—its compound with
hydrogen is CH_4, the common marsh gas, methane. Only the
combination of H and O produces a liquid. Why? The answer
lies in the anatomy of the molecule, the shape that it takes, and
the kind of energy that binds its two parts together. Water is a
lopsided molecule, the oxygen binding one H tightly to form an
OH combination that carries a negative charge, and the other
H more loosely retaining at this "pole" a positive charge. We say
that the water molecule is dipolar, having a + at one end and a
− at the other. The strength of the bonding is difficult to
measure, but it is strong and is called covalent. In addition, the
kind of bond that holds otherwise separate water molecules
together are basically "hydrogen bonds," about which chemists
still have much to learn, but which are of great significance in
most biologically important compounds.

Indeed, the hydrogen bonds allow water molecules to form
more or less loose aggregates with each other. Being dipoles,

and remember that opposite charges attract whereas like charges repel, water molecules associate in twos and threes forming little clusters that are then too large and dense to fly off into the atmosphere as gas. It takes a great deal of energy to break these hydrogen bonds. Since heat is energy it follows that much heat is required to warm water and even more to evaporate water—or as chemists say, the "heat of vaporization" is high. That is why water is liquid, and remains liquid over the range of temperatures that normally prevail on earth.

The lopsided form of the water molecule becomes especially important when we examine what happens when water is cooled. Like all other substances, water shrinks or contracts on cooling —that is, down to a point. Then, suddenly, just a few degrees above freezing (4°C or 39°F) it begins to *expand* and does so until the freezing point is reached. This is a remarkable and *wholly unique* phenomenon. No other material behaves this way and it is of incalculable importance to life. Suppose for a moment that water did not expand (about 9 per cent of its volume) on freezing. This might be good for water pipes, but it would mean that ice, instead of floating, would sink. Since heat penetrates only a little into water, ice on the bottom of lakes and streams and oceans would never melt, would accumulate each year during winter's cold, and soon Earth would be uninhabitable! The important all-essential expansion of cold water results from the same lopsided-dipole molecules that aggregate into a hexagonal crystal pattern occupying 9 per cent more space than cool liquid —and permits life to continue.

Many other properties of water are unique and important for life. Of these let us mention only one more: the remarkable power of water to dissolve other materials. Water will hold in solution more substances than any material known, it is nearly a universal solvent, and its remarkable dissolving powers make water the medium for all the biochemical reactions on which continued life depends.

Water is important, mighty important. How much of it is

there? About 9 million billion tons. That is about 324 million cubic miles in all the oceans, lakes, rivers, and streams, about 2 billion cubic miles more in ground water, and another 3,100 cubic miles in the atmosphere. And there is a constant cycling from atmosphere to Earth's surface. Annually there fall upon this Earth about 10^{17} gallons of rain; that is about 100 million billion gallons, or 30 inches everywhere, if it all fell uniformly. Should all the water on Earth be heaped upon the United States, it would cover us to a depth of 90 miles; if it covered a uniform Earth evenly it would be everywhere about $2\frac{1}{4}$ miles deep. There is a lot of water, but it is not distributed equally. The 3,100 cubic miles of atmospheric water is fully discharged about every 12 days, but not equitably.

What I wish to emphasize now is that, first, there is a great amount of water and that it cycles and recycles continuously. This has been going on since Earth began; it will not stop tomorrow, nor in our lifetime. Second, water is not uniformly distributed—witness the oceans and the land. Third, water has great solvent properties: no natural body of water is "pure," and only "fresh" water is potable. Substances, chemical and biological, have been finding their way into water for millions of years; this also will continue.

We cannot "use up" water. There is the same amount of water today as 3 billion years ago. Sometimes water is locked up—in glaciers for centuries, in the bodies of animals or plants for years or decades—but all water eventually cycles and the water balance is constant. Yesterday and today and tomorrow the total amount of water remains the same.

Two things *are* of concern, however: the *uneven distribution* of water and what gets *dissolved* or suspended in it. Let us recognize that there are wetlands, there are areas of adequate or moderate rainfall, and there are deserts. The last are unfit for human habitation unless water is brought in—usually at great expense and from a great distance. The folly of trying to colonize the desert without imposing a user's tax for water is so self-evident that it does not merit comment. But the problems of conveying

water to where people are—or conversely, the shifting of populations or agriculture or industry to where water is—is a problem
worthy of study. Transporting fresh water is costly, but it is tech-
nically possible. It was done by all of the great dead civilizations
of the past.

Of greater interest to us is, I think, the question of what is dissolved in water—the problem of water pollution. Remember
here that pollution itself is a relative term. We consider biological wastes to be pollutants in water only if they come from human beings or land animals—we care little about the excreta of
the aquatic community. Yet fish and worms and insects and all
manner of plants live out their lives in water; indeed, fresh-water
fish can survive *only* because their kidneys are hyperactive,
secreting copious quantities of hypotonic urine! Biological
wastes, including human sewage, have cycled through water
from time immemorial—this is no recent innovation—but it is
only lately that *large quantities* have inundated and overwhelmed
the natural processes of change to the point where the very
sources of water are polluted. Add to the biological wastes those
from chemical fertilizers in agriculture, from industry, and from
the introduction of novel substances (from DDT to detergents)
never known in the world before, and we begin to define the
outline of our present problem. Does this mean we must wring
our hands and wail that we've done wrong? By no means. It is
time to stop the self-flagellation that holds man to be little more
than the meanest beast; it is time to have the courage to accept,
with proper humility and in the spirit of the nobler aspirations
of the human mind, our responsibility for the stewardship of
this planet. No longer can we rely upon the automatic cleansing
of the Earth's waters by cycling through the large natural system; we must take a hand in that cycling ourselves. I propose
two things worth studying.

1. The establishment of priorities for water use, that is, human
consumption, washing and bathing, food and other processing,
mineral processing and industry, and consideration of the recycling of water *separately* for each of these uses. Each kind of

use demands a different type of treatment for reuse; a city should think anew about its water supply being multipurpose.

2. The development of ways to speed up the purification of already polluted natural bodies of water. It has to come, so let us get started. And in all of this, forget that water is free—it is our most precious commodity.

CHALLENGE FOR SURVIVAL *Commentary*

by Franklin S. Forsberg

I would like to speak with you today for a few moments as though I were speaking with some of our eight million readers. So please accept me into your confidence as a recreationist, not as a scientist. Of great interest to us in our editorial approach to our readers is the conservation of water for recreational purposes. Because water has always been plentiful and easily available in America, it is not here the precious substance many other people of the world consider it to be. Americans feel that the price of water is so low that to promote economy in its use is not feasible. The older communities of Europe hold that the amount of fresh water available depends upon the price people are willing to pay for it. And speaking of price, it has been calculated that the average American family spends about three dollars a month for water and fifteen dollars each month for alcoholic beverages.

The recreational uses of water include not only boating, fishing, swimming, scuba diving, water skiing, and surfing, but also the esthetic value of a body of water that is pleasant to the eye, to the nose, and suitable for camping or picnicking.

There may be as many as seven million skin and scuba divers in the United States. There will be ten million individuals water skiing in the country this summer. Swimming is growing in popularity at such a rate that it may become the number one outdoor activity in America by 1980. In 1965, a Department of the Interior study reveals, there were nine hundred and seventy million individual participations in swimming. This means the average American, from toddler to grandparent, goes swimming about five times a year. Swimming alone is going to consume a lot of water from the total amount that will be available for the next few decades. There are more than a half million residential swimming pools in the United States, and the number is increasing at the rate of over a thousand per week. This is in addition to the more than twenty thousand new swimming pools being built each year for hotels, motels, apartments, and schools.

Americans spend more money each year on boats than they do on books. There were forty thousand new canoes and sailboats, plus more than a thousand houseboats, added to the increasing fleet of pleasure craft last year. There are eight and a half million boats of all kinds used for recreation in the United States. From industry figures we estimate that there are forty thousand surf boards in use this year. And there was an increase of nearly 30 per cent in this activity in 1967. With more than eight million boat owners, seven million skin and scuba divers, ten million water skiers, forty thousand surfers, sixty-eight million swimmers, and countless millions of others who use the waters of the nation for fishing and other outdoor activities, I think it is safe to assume that every individual in the United States has a personal stake in water for recreation.

Dovetailed with this fact is the increase in non-working time and the fairly finite amount of water available for all purposes. The Hudson Institute projections of American life into the twenty-first century suggest—and I hope that some of them endure—that the work week will gradually become shortened to less than thirty-five hours by 1985 and to about thirty hours by the year 2,000. In addition, there will obviously be more paid holidays and longer vacations, as well as earlier retirements. The employed man of the year 2,000 may actually spend only eleven hundred hours a year at his job, compared to today's standard of nineteen hundred hours. The American worker, even after nineteen hundred hours on the job, finds plenty of time for boating, swimming, and other forms of outdoor recreation. Given an extra eight hundred hours, or twenty full work weeks of free time a year, much additional time is going to be spent in the recreational use of water.

We find water-oriented commuters in all parts of the country. When the American breadwinner can have his choice, he will make his home near a body of water. And when he retires, he selects a retirement site near the water. Hardly anyone, to my knowledge, plans to retire to an apartment across the street from the public library.

Little consideration has been given thus far to the quality and the quantity of water needed for recreational purposes. For example, we mentioned earlier that federal statistics show about sixty-eight million swimmers participating in the sport for a total of nearly one billion times each year. But what standards of water quality do we have for swimming in lakes, rivers, oceans, and elsewhere? One expert has stated his answer to this question in a very obvious way: since swimmers usually drink some of the water they swim in, they should swim in drinking water. This would be an ideal situation, but water of drinking-quality is hard to achieve, even in a swimming pool. Sewage-polluted sea water is considered satisfactory for swimmers, as long as the fecal matter is properly disintegrated and the water is not esthetically revolting. The source of much sewage is the treatment plants of municipalities along the waterways. It is more economical simply to dump sewage than to give it a full treatment. The municipal sanitation department has performed and fulfilled its legal requirement; but from the viewpoint of the skier and other users of the water, the level of pollution has hardly been touched.

I would like to cite just one example of the paradox of pollution control. The Federal Water Pollution Control Administration reported last year that in one community a chemical was applied to water near a beach to make it safe for swimming. Using the same rule that many of us do, that twice as much of the chemical would make the beach twice as safe, the dose was doubled. As a result the beach was not suitable for swimmers, because it was littered with the rotten carcasses of fish killed by disinfectant. This is but one of the hundreds of examples which have come to our attention of damage to the recreational value of water when a local effort to solve an immediate problem is not coordinated with the interests of other groups needing the water for different purposes.

On the other hand, there are kinds of pollution which have been unfairly attributed to the recreational users of water, for example, sewage disposal from pleasure boats. Although it has been popular in recent years to blame small-boat operators for contamination of water, it can be proved in nearly every instance that the major source of the pollution has been a nearby municipal sewage treatment plant. Boat owners have been accused of polluting the Hudson River, although there are fewer than two thousand boats on the Hudson that are equipped with heads. Over the whole country there are, at the most, about six hundred thousand pleasure boats with heads—and this represents only about 7 per cent of the total number of registered boats within the United States. One industry survey indicates that boats are responsible for less than one-half of one per cent of the sewage pollution of our waters. Hence, we in recreation do not like to assume the blame for pollution. All of the boats in Connecticut constitute less of a pollution threat to Long Island Sound than the sewage outflow from a single small community that uses the ocean as its ultimate sewer. Let me point out that no group that I know of is more concerned about the welfare of the nation's water than the boaters.

Boat owners probably would move much more quickly to control their own pollution if it were not for the myriad of conflicting laws and regulations. The matter of oil pollution of our waters is another example of the pleasure-boat owner being a scapegoat although he contributes little of the contamination. The main sources of oil pollution are the spillage at shipyards, oil terminals, and what Secretary Udall described as "the sloppy habits and poor standards of the shipping industry."

The job ahead is an immense one. Water management from the local to the federal level must be a cooperative effort, joined by the committees of articulate people and the business community. Perhaps we will never eliminate the waste accumulation in our waters. But we must not deny the usage by legitimate consumers. We should have by now marked the turning point in national consciousness of water pollution. I am afraid we have not.

A large part of our problem is the assimilation of facts and then their intelligent communication. We, in the communications business, are hungry for articulate, factual, consumer-oriented material to transmit to the general public. We assume that the present threat to our environment is as serious as a disease epidemic. But thus far, we have been able to conduct a war only on paper. And until we are able to stimulate the public to take action, this symposium will have been only a meeting of people rather than a meeting of minds.

One more disturbing factor is the lack of action-directed responsibility. And here is my challenge to this group: The meeting could go into the histories of conservation as the turning point in man's effort to stop the suicidal destruction of the natural resources. If we permit this meeting to adjourn without taking some positive action toward an effective solution of our environmental deterioration, it will mean simply that this has been another academic exercise. However, we do have assembled in this room some of the most influential men and women of science and letters as well as educators and communicators. This is truly a people's war, and when we consider the alternative the choice is clear. May I make the plea—let's take the problem out of the classroom and put it in the boardroom and in the family room.

Our freshwater environment

RUTH PATRICK

Since the nomads roamed the deserts, today, and for a long time to come, fresh water—that is, water suitable for whatever use man wants to make of it—has been our continual quest. Its importance to man through the ages is seen in the legends and rites of many tribes. Today it is a central problem in legislative, governmental, and industrial bodies.

Fresh water means many things to many people. To some it means the lake—a place to water ski or sail. To others it is a stream to fish in or simply a pleasant place near which to walk and think. Only recently has the recreational use of water had such high priority. When man worked from sun to sun, he had little time to water ski or fish or even take a walk along a wooded stream, but with our shorter work week recreation has become big business. In Pennsylvania it is now our second largest industry. Indeed, recreation is producing its own water-pollution problems, because so many people are indulging in water activities during their free hours.

In former days rivers meant power to many people. It was the force of the streams that ran the mills or the hydroelectric power plants. To others it meant navigation, drinking water, or a place to discharge wastes. Although some of the major uses change with time, water is still of major concern to all. In spite of the

Reprinted from *Garden Journal* 18(6): 174–176, 1968; lightly edited.

fact that the freshwater world is so important to our daily life, relatively few men have looked beneath the water's surface to determine how its ecosystems function and how they are able to recover from the perturbation that man causes.

As in the terrestrial world there are many kinds of organisms functioning in an aquatic ecosystem, which has four or five stages of energy transfer. These are the decomposers (organisms which break up organic materials and detritus); algae, which are plants that fix the sun's energy; animals such as insects and snails, commonly called herbivores, that feed upon the plants; and animals which we call carnivores that feed upon each other. But the kinds of organisms of the aquatic world are very different from those in the terrestrial world, although some of them belong to the same major groups.

The bacteria and aquatic fungi take the wastes which enter the water and break them up into simple chemical forms that can be utilized directly as food by the plants known as algae and in some instances by animals such as protozoa (Patrick 1951). The bacteria, in breaking down these complex organic compounds, use up oxygen in their metabolism. The more bacteria that are formed and the more wastes that are broken down, the more oxygen is used up. Indeed, the oxygen would become exhausted if it were not for the aquatic plants, which are mainly algae. These plants, by the process of photosynthesis, fix carbon and at the same time produce oxygen, thus restoring to the water oxygen that is used up by the bacteria and all other organisms in respiration. The only other source of oxygen is the atmosphere, but usually this is not so effective a way of reoxygenating a body of water as is photosynthesis. The algae, if they are the right species, are also excellent food for the aquatic animals in our ecosystem, just as the grasses of the meadows are the best type of food for any animals in our terrestrial world.

Protozoa, which are one-celled organisms (some people consider them acellular), feed upon the bacteria. Indeed, the bacteria would become too numerous and thus kill themselves by the production of autotoxins if it were not for the protozoa that feed upon them and keep their populations in check, thus helping them perform the function of decomposition most effectively. Other decomposers are the fungi. We know little about the aquatic fungi, but we do know they play an important role in the breaking up of detritus. As I stated earlier, the algae are the main food for most forms of aquatic life. The insects and many of the invertebrates as well as the protozoa feed upon the algae. These organisms are known as herbivores. Fish, too, may be herbivores. Most of the larger animals in the aquatic and terrestrial worlds are herbivores, because there is enough fixed energy to nourish them only at the base of the food chain. This is particularly true if they typically have large populations. The herbivores are fed upon by other animals, such as some of the insects or fish. It is interesting to note that most of the major groups of animals contain species which are herbivores, carnivores, and omnivores.

In the aquatic world as in the terrestrial world there are many paths in the food web, and there are many species at each stage of this food web or system of energy transfer. Likewise, the paths of energy through this ecosystem are varied. Some of the energy flows from the decomposers to the plants and back to the decomposers, whereas other energy is transferred through herbivores and back to decomposers. Longer paths are taken by potential energy molecules that go from the decomposers to algae to herbivores to carnivores and, should secondary carnivores be present, through them before being returned to the decomposer. We do not know much about the relative amounts of energy that pass through these various cycles, but we do know that such cycles exist, and probably there is a delicate balance which determines the efficiency of the functioning of the ecosystem.

This aquatic ecosystem is a carefully balanced, closely knit community. I often like to compare it to an orchestra. There are many instruments or organisms, each playing a different part, and each one must play its part correctly if the ecosystem is to function naturally, as in an orchestra each instrument must play its part correctly and with the right intensity if the beauty of the symphony is to be preserved. If any instrument gets out of balance or if any organisms are eliminated in this complex food web, the system is altered and, if the change is great enough, destroyed. The natural and proper functioning of this ecosystem is the means by which a river or lake cleanses itself and maintains its natural beauty and usefulness for many purposes.

We have found through research that natural, healthy ecosystems consist of many species, and most of these species have relatively small populations (Patrick 1949). The actual number will vary according to the type of lake or stream. Furthermore, in any given environment these numbers of species composing the ecosystem remain quite similar from season to season and from year to year. The kinds of species may vary greatly, but they are replaced by species with similar ecological requirements and with similar functions (Patrick 1961).

The disturbances resulting from pollution may affect natural or healthy ecosystems in many ways. Some species may increase somewhat in numbers whereas others decrease. For example, protozoan species which feed upon bacteria may increase in number if the bacterial load is unusually large. More often, however, one of the main effects of pollution is that it causes certain tolerant species to be more common—in other words, those species that can tolerate the type of disturbance or imbalance created by pollution are opportunistic and take advantage of beneficial effects produced. At the same time those species that cannot tolerate the new ecological regime become more scarce. The predator pressure typically does not rise so fast as the population size; thus, a large standing crop results as one of the first effects of mild pollution. However, if the pollution becomes more severe, the numbers of species drop; indeed, if the pollution is toxic or inimical to aquatic life, then the species reduce without any increase in size of populations.

The general kinds of pollution which may enter a stream because of man's activities are suspended solids, toxic pollutants, organic pollutants, and heat (Patrick 1953, 1962). The most obvious effect of a suspended-solids load is to reduce light penetration into the water. Light is important for the process of photosynthesis, which produces oxygen and thus replaces the oxygen used by respiration. Our studies have shown that most organisms live in the photosynthetic zone. Therefore, if the photosynthetic zone is reduced, the area for species occupancy is also reduced for most animals.

The larger particles of the *suspended-solids* load settle out relatively quickly and clog up the habitats of organisms, thus reducing the heterogeneity of the environment. The smaller particulate matter is often carried downstream and remains suspended as long as the current is relatively swift. This smaller particulate matter often serves as a substrate for bacteria, and it is known that under a given degree of organic enrichment water containing suspended solids may often support more bacteria than clear water of a similar nutrient level. The colloids, which are the very small particles in the suspended-solids load, act in many different ways. Perhaps their most important characteristic is that their surfaces are electrically active and thus can adsorb many different kinds of ions. If the ions available are important nutrient ions, the colloids may act as a reservoir for nutrients. A chemical test, therefore, may show the water to be relatively low in nutrients where in actuality a fair amount of nutrients available for plant life is adsorbed upon the surface of these colloidal mycelia. In a similar way these colloidal particles may act as a reservoir for toxic materials, and thus heavy metals or radioactive materials may be adsorbed onto the surface of these colloids and carried along the stream. They are only deposited where these colloids settle out, and this may be many miles downstream.

Toxic materials, if very toxic or in a relatively large concentration, may kill in a very short time the aquatic life which is present. More difficult to diagnose are those materials which are in smaller concentrations or are less toxic but produce a chronic toxic effect. Experiments in our laboratories have shown that some organic chemical toxins in very small amounts affect the breeding behavior of fish, causing the male fish to fail to chase the female or to stake out a territory. These latter types of toxicants which affect the behavior or metabolism of fish, although they do not immediately kill the individual, will in the long run eliminate the species.

Organic pollution, which arises mainly from sewage treatment plants and from cattle and hog feedlots, usually affects the aquatic community by producing excessive amounts of nutrients or by changing the balance of nutrients, thus often favoring undesirable species. An example of this is the development of *Cladophora*, *Stigeoclonium*, or bluegreen algae in polluted areas. Because these algae are not desirable sources of food, the predators in a stream will either not feed upon them or feed upon them very inefficiently and thus the predators will eventually be eliminated. As a result, a large standing algae crop develops which we call a nuisance growth. A similar amount of nutrients flowing through species such as diatoms, which have a high predator pressure, will cause high productivity of herbivores and in turn carnivores, and thus a natural river will result that has high productivity rather than one that is esthetically unpleasing and not productive of the higher stages in the food web.

The effects of *temperature* are many and varied, both direct and indirect. Examples of indirect effects are the increase in solubility of certain compounds and their diffusion. The more direct effects are those that limit the functioning of the organism. Too high temperatures, such as those greater than 90°–93°F, may immediately produce death. Likewise, too great or too sudden a change in temperature may bring about the death of individuals. High temperatures often affect the rate of metabolism. For example, in a series of experiments which we were carrying out, we gradually raised the temperature so that catfish could live and tolerate it, but their respiration rate went up so fast that they could not assimilate food rapidly enough, and thus they starved to death although plenty of food was available.

A change of temperature is known to be necessary for the reproduction of many organisms. Oysters in the middle Atlantic states, for example, in order to spawn must have water that passes from the low to mid 60°s F to a little above 70°F. Likewise, to spawn in Maryland bass must have temperatures that pass from the low 60°s to the high 60°s F in order for them to breed. The molting of insects is often triggered by a change in temperature. High temperatures over long periods of time may promote diseases of various types in aquatic organisms.

Thus we see that perturbation produced by pollution may greatly alter the efficiency of a natural aquatic system. Perhaps the most severe effect of perturbation is the long-range one which results in a great reduction in the diversity of species composing man's environment, and this in turn reduces the flexibility of the aquatic communities to adjust to changing conditions. Once this flexibility is destroyed, it is extremely difficult to restore it.

As we look into the future it is evident that there are going to be more and more people working shorter periods of time. This means that man is going to demand more and more of the surface waters for recreational use and at the same time more material things for his way of life.

Our challenges on a nationwide or worldwide basis are first to improve our methods of manufacturing so that waste products are greatly reduced and second to re-use water and solid wastes more efficiently. Today we are a "once through nation," but tomorrow we must become a "re-use nation." Disposal at sea and underground are only temporary measures.

We must also, I believe, attack the pollution problem in quite another way. We should realize the fact that probably all pollution will not be removed from our lakes and streams even though mankind does all he can do to prevent pollution from entering them. Realizing this, we must learn: (*a*) how to plan the use of a watershed so that natural areas which can support high species diversity characteristic of the area are maintained, and (*b*) how to manage our streams in areas of heavy stream usage so that they will produce the kinds of species we desire and so that the pattern of energy and/or nutrient flow will be one that promotes stability. It is well known that the agriculturist or horticulturist conducts a soil test and adds nutrients to the soil to balance out those that are present in order to grow desirable crops. This same philosophy may be one which we will wish to follow in stream management—that is, in order to balance out the nutrients in some instances it may be desirable to add minute amounts of certain substances such as manganese or vitamin B^{12} to promote species that have a high predator-prey ratio and desirable productivity rather than to allow nutrient imbalances to occur that result in nuisance algae growths (Patrick 1968).

Another approach I believe we will follow in the future is to actually architect our streams in areas of heavy usage—that is, to create shallow water areas with the correct kinds of substrates and current structures to encourage the growth of desirable food species for the food web of the aquatic ecosystem. As we learn more about the requirements of the desirable species of aquatic life and how to interrelate these requirements through systems analyses, we will be able to design and construct what is necessary for their best growth.

I believe the ingenuity of man will find ways to have use without abuse of our surface waters. However, man must come face-to-face with what he wants for his material way of life and what price he is willing to pay for good water.

REFERENCES

Patrick, R. 1949. A proposed biological measure of stream conditions based on a survey of the Conestoga Basin, Lancaster County, Pennsylvania. *Proc. Acad. Nat. Sci. Philadelphia* 101:277–341.

Patrick, R. 1951. A proposed biological measure of stream conditions. *Proc. Int. Assoc. Theoretical and Applied Limnology* 11:299–307.

Patrick, R. 1953. Biological phases of stream pollution. *Proc. Pennsylvania Acad. Sci.* 27:33–66.

Patrick, R. 1961. A study of the numbers and kinds of species found in rivers in eastern United States. *Proc. Acad. Nat. Sci. Philadelphia* 113(10): 215–258.

Patrick, R. 1962. Effects of river physical and chemical characteristics on aquatic life. *Jour. American Water Works Assoc.* 54(3):546–550.

CHALLENGE FOR SURVIVAL *Commentary*

by Edward R. Trapnell

Being called upon for a commentary on Dr. Patrick's paper, "Our freshwater environment," I am happy to respond to my program assignment. If I were to put a short title on Dr. Patrick's paper, it would be something like "These Busy Waters," because one has no idea what is going on all the time in water that appears to be clear and undisturbed. I must say, Dr. Patrick, it is an encouraging paper. At least, I hope you meant it to be encouraging. That is my reaction. Even if you had not intended that we take constructive comfort from your discussion, you have made a great contribution to our understanding of what is going on in the flowing stream and how we can make use of what might be called the in-stream processing capabilities of our rivers.

The process you have described brings to mind an analogy with the construction business. We constantly see huge transit-mix concrete trucks moving through the streets. This is what is going on in our rivers. We are using them for a kind of transit-mix operation: to transport our wastes, both industrial and domestic, and to process them in transit. We've made a science of mixing cement in transit and delivering it to a construction site, having it arrive just when it is needed and when it is ready to pour. This is a very carefully programmed operation, as our computer-minded friends would say. The amount of ingredients put in is adjusted to the capacity of the mixer tank. The rate of input of the water and the mixing are scheduled and controlled. We do it every day and think nothing of it. It works nicely.

Somehow, we haven't given much thought to doing this with our rivers. Perhaps we can learn from the ecologists or the limnologists. We ought to be able to find the transit-mix capacity of a river. Then we could adjust the sewage input or condition it in such a way that the in-stream processing of the river stays in balance. The river would have an opportunity to complete the process before it reaches the next downstream city to be tapped again for drinking water.

We really don't have much choice in this matter. We have to learn to take better care of and make better use of our water resources. The thing we have to realize, the hard truth we have to face, is that the amount of water available to us is fixed and our demand for it is not. The amount of water in the Earth biosphere is constant. It has never been any more or less than it is now or will be in the future. But the number of people that have to use it and the way they use it are not fixed in any way. There is an equilibrium here that we must define and reach.

Of course, the water we have is not always distributed the way we'd like it to be. People sometimes seem to want to live where water isn't, and they often don't want to live where the water is. Without going into all the reasons, we can see that there are more people in Southern California and Arizona than there are in the Yukon and the Northwest Territories of Canada. The urge of some engineers of The Ralph M. Parsons Company to do something about this seeming perverseness of man in his relationship with nature led to the North American Water and Power Alliance (NAWAPA) concept (Parsons Company, 1964).

This is a plan, or a concept, of continent-wide scope, to take some of the water flowing unused into the Arctic and to redistribute it over the continent to places where we can make better use of it. The areas to be benefited would be the southern tier of the Prairie Provinces of Canada; the whole of the Great Lakes Basin and its surrounding basins; and the semi-arid lands of the high plains, the southwestern states of the United States, and northern Mexico.

There is a question I want to ask, but before doing so let me make one point about NAWAPA. It has no official status, of course; the name was selected by the developers. The idea is being increasingly studied with many variations. Whatever may emerge, the Parsons work has stimulated a whole new approach to water-resource planning and has demonstrated both the technical and economic feasibility of continent-wide water resource development.

Some half-dozen variations on the NAWAPA theme have been published in recent years. None is quite so extensive as the Parsons concept. The continental water redistribution system and the power network envisioned by Parsons would cost $100 billion and take twenty-five years to build. Its designers say it would pay out on the same basis as many existing water and power projects in all three countries.

The point I want to make is that it doesn't make sense to talk about such a distribution system without first tending to the production side of the business. This means a greatly expanded and more intensive conservation effort in all of the water harvest areas of the continent. Water is a crop, and if we take care of the fields, they will keep on producing. Water doesn't have to be a depletable resource. Like timber, it can be a sustained-yield crop. Furthermore, both the production and the distribution requirements will be served by adequate pollution control. We will have to clean up the natural water courses used in the distribution scheme. In other words, both conservation and pollution control are prerequisites of the massive transfer projects envisioned in true continental water resource development.

One of the principal benefits of all of these proposals is augmentation of the Great Lakes, one of which is Lake Erie. I will close with a question. Are we doing enough in the way of research to learn how to design the streams or to manage them in such a way that they can do the transit-mix job? The specific focus of my question is Lake Erie, since augmentation of the Great Lakes is one of the features of the continental system. Do we know enough now to save Lake Erie or are we on the way to acquiring the knowledge? With effective pollution control and new water, would it be possible to restore Lake Erie to water health?

REFERENCE

NAWAPA is an engineering plan developed by The Ralph M. Parsons Company and published by the company in April, 1964. The original version, since expanded and slightly revised, was studied and discussed in detail in a report on Western Water Development, A Summary of Water Resources Projects, Plans and Studies Relating to The Western and Midwestern United States. Compiled by the Special Committee on Western Water Development of the Committee On Public Works, United States Senate, this report was published as a Committee Print in October 1964 by the U.S. Government Printing Office. Copies of the Subcommittee report and additional materials on NAWAPA are available from the Parsons offices at 617 West Seventh St., Los Angeles, Calif. 90017, and at 1000 16th St., Washington, D.C. 20036.

The ecology of wetlands in urban areas WILLIAM A. NIERING

Man is a threatened species. The twin specters facing him are over-population and unbridled technology—both self-induced.

The double threat is aimed most directly at man's environment. As the United States strives to accommodate more human beings than it has ever had to serve before, increased demands are placed on our natural resource bank. Our surroundings become increasingly crowded, noisy, and soiled.

These opening paragraphs from the Department of the Interior Conservation Yearbook, *Man . . . an endangered species?*, echo the grave concern being expressed by certain federal agencies and Congressmen on the Washington scene. As a nation we have in the twentieth century reached a high level of affluence, but the environmental price of this progress has been high. Accelerated eutrophication of our lakes and rivers, so polluted they occasionally catch fire, has prompted the enactment of federal water-pollution control legislation. But our rapid stride to opulence has also had a drastic impact on other natural landscapes, namely the wetlands. Although the nation's marshes, swamps, and bogs are among the most productive landscapes in the world, these liquid assets have suffered greater destruction and abuse than any other natural habitat manipulated by man. As a result of draining, dredging, filling, and/or pollution we have

Reprinted from *Garden Journal* 18(6): 177–183, 1968; lightly edited.

in the conterminous United States reduced the nation's wetland asset to 70 million acres, slightly more than half the original acreage (an estimated 127 million acres). And the destruction is continuing at an accelerated pace of 1 per cent or more per year, favored by the pseudo-socio-economic concept that conversion of these habitats into other land-use patterns results in the highest and best use. Unfortunately, such decisions have usually been conceived in narrow economic terms with no critical evaluation of the significant ecological role such areas serve in the community, the state, or the broader national interest.

It is in this context and that of our symposium "Challenge for Survival" that I should like briefly to examine the ecological role of the wetlands, the impact of man on their ecology, and the action which must be taken to safeguard these assets.

THEIR ECOLOGICAL ROLE

In the urban–suburban complex the remaining wetlands are engulfed by some 140 million Americans crowded onto less than 5 per cent of the land. Yet cattail marshes, wooded swamps, and fringing tidal marshes can still persist if given adequate protection from the environmental stresses of urbanization. Unfortunately, to the average urban dweller such areas appear to have little relevance to daily life. For this reason a review of the ecological role these wetlands serve may be enlightening (Niering 1966).

Hydrology. Wetlands are of major importance in the nation's hydrologic regime. Because of their water-holding capacity they act as storage basins assisting in minimizing erosion and serving to reduce the destruction of floods. In cities this is especially important, because urbanization intensifies the rate of runoff as buildings, concrete, and asphalt tend to concentrate large volumes of precipitation. Since cities are deficient in soak-in areas, the runoff is usually rapid and in excessive volumes. Wetlands, including floodplains, act as catchment basins and tend to slow the speed of flow, thus minimizing flood damage. In 1955 when the severe floods struck eastern Pennsylvania, hundreds of bridges were washed out along the stream courses. However, two bridges of the type destroyed were left standing below the Cranberry Bog, a natural area preserved by the Nature Conservancy. Floodplains also represent a hydrologic feature ideally designed to carry water during peak flows. Every effort should be made to maintain these valley landscapes free of developments, restricting them for recreation or those activities not incompatible with periodic flooding.

Furthermore, wetlands are important oxidation and sedimentation basins where tons of organic and inorganic sediments are deposited from the urban runoff. Although accelerating eutrophication when intercepted by marshes and swamps, the organic component is slowly oxidized, and the nutrients are made available to the wetland ecosystems rather than being flushed into rivers and streams or the local sewage system.

Marine productivity. Turning to the coastal wetlands, we see that tidal marshes represent an important marine resource rapidly being engulfed by development. Extremely limited in extent, these fringing wetlands are delicately balanced ecosystems that grow upward and landward, keeping pace with the constantly rising sea level. Although most of the rise was completed 5,000 years ago, it is still occurring at the rate of about three inches per century along the Atlantic shoreline. In response to a complex of factors involving salinity, there have also developed distinctive belts of marsh vegetation as one progresses from the estuary to the upper marsh border. Located at the break in the slope and at the tidal–fresh water interface, sediments not only tend to accumulate but nutrients also concentrate. Therefore, the marsh–estuarine system is one of the most productive in the world. In a Georgia salt marsh it has been reported that seven times more protein is produced than in the best Kansas wheat field. Here the food web begins that supports our coastal fisheries. Algae and detritus from the marsh grasses nourish the shellfish. The abundance of plankton and crustaceans provides food for small fish (such as menhaden) that are consumed by flounder, striped bass, and blue-fish. These in turn support our spectacular game fish—tuna, marlin, sword-fish, and sailfish. Here too are the nursery grounds for two dozen or more commercially important crustacea, shellfish, and finfish. In fact, it is estimated that 90 per cent of the total harvest of seafood taken by American fishermen is caught on the Continental shelf; about two-thirds of these species are dependent in part on the marsh–estuarine ecosystem.

Tidal marshes are geologically significant as sediment accretors. When marshes are destroyed, those sediments that are normally deposited on the marsh in its upward growth end up in channels, necessitating constant dredging. The organic carpets of peat and marsh grasses also exhibit great resiliency in buffering the shoreline during periodic storms, giving the upland an added degree of protection.

Duck factories. Although the nation's midwest pothole country produces over 50 per cent of our ducks, the eastern coastal marshes around suburbia produce 200,000 and the southern states another 700,000 during the best years. Even though those in the west are the most significant as breeding areas, all are important —including those in and around cities that serve as vital resting and feeding grounds during migration. New York's Jamaica Bay is an excellent example. It should also be recognized that, where one is dealing with a migrating resource, those wetlands serving as breeding grounds can affect the waterfowl population and ultimately the hunter or naturalist thousands of miles away.

Education and recreation. Wetlands are outdoor educational and scientific laboratories. They furnish the resources for scientific research and serve as living museums for teaching the dynamics and ecological role these systems serve. At the Connecticut Arboretum the permanently preserved wetlands have been variously explored by Connecticut College students. A red-maple swamp, actually a bog, with its underlying 20 feet of peat served as a challenging problem to an undergraduate as she unravelled the 13,000 years of post-glacial forest history revealed by the pollen preserved in the peat. The Mamacoke tidal-marsh salinities studies have been conducted in an effort to better understand marsh zonation, and permanent mapping studies will reveal future changes in the marsh vegetation. At the Thames Science Center, closely affiliated with the Arboretum, thousands of school children annually are given first-hand field experience and are being taught the value of wetlands. The Arboretum Guided Tour used by the teachers makes its point about the wetland along the route. "The swamp below this dam is roughly an acre in size. If flooded to a depth of one foot it would hold 330,000 gallons of water. Thus whenever a swamp is filled or drained another large quantity of water is lost from the underground water supply and made to run off more quickly to aggravate flooding problems down stream."

Wetlands also provide many recreational outlets such as fishing, hunting, bird watching, or hiking. Twenty million Americans go fishing, two million hunt waterfowl. Thousands hunt with binoculars and cameras where an unparalleled diversity of waterfowl and spectacular marsh birds gives pleasure and inspiration. On Staten Island a unique fenway system has been proposed for incorporating the wetlands as part of the open-space pattern. It represents a sound ecological use of resources, and the recreation potential is unlimited. Such a mosaic of open space serves as an essential structure to any developing community. It performs an important social function and greatly enhances the quality of the environment.

THE IMPACT OF MAN

Filling, dredging, and draining. In *The Merchant of Venice*, Shakespeare wrote: "You take my life when you take the means whereby I live." Wetland destruction as a result of filling, dredging, and draining has been widespread, especially in highly developed areas. Tidal marshes on the south shore of Long Island Sound have been reduced from 30,000 to 16,000 acres. Similarly, along the Connecticut shoreline almost half (45 per cent) of the

36.5 square miles of salt marshes found in the state in 1914 had been destroyed by 1959; at the present rate of destruction, 14 per cent will remain by the year 2000. At Sherwood Island State Park, Westport, Connecticut, 3.5 million cubic yards of gravel were taken from Long Island Sound by hydraulic dredging. Much of this gravel was used in the construction of the Connecticut Turnpike; the remainder obliterated the life of a marsh to create a parking area. Even the site of Kennedy International Airport was once a productive marsh.

Dredging and draining operations can also drastically affect the ecology of wetlands. Dredging causes increased turbidity which decreases light reaching photosynthetic organisms at the base of the food chain. Filter feeders such as shellfish may be adversely affected or actually killed. Suitable hard surfaces for the attachment of larval stages of shellfish may be covered by excessive sediment. The adverse biological effects on wildlife as a result of widespread tidal-marsh ditching for mosquito control along the Atlantic coast are well documented. In Delaware natural marsh grasses were replaced by two shrubby species: marsh elder and groundsel. Mollusk and crustacean populations, important food of water fowl and other marsh birds, were reduced up to 95 per cent.

In Florida, drainage operations by large corporate developers are threatening the future of Corkscrew Swamp, a magnificent mature cypress forest owned by the National Audubon Society.

One only needs to look within his own community to see where the sanitary land-fill operations are occurring to realize that wetlands are still regarded as wastelands.

Even those wetlands dedicated as natural preserves are being continuously subjected to encroachment. Troy Meadows is a classic example. Located 20 airline miles from Times Square in Morris County, New Jersey, this 3,000-acre marsh, half of which is held as a wildlife refuge by Wildlife Preserves, Inc., is now being subjected to the following encroachments: two transmission right-of-ways, two gas pipe lines, four sewer lines, a pumping station, three water wells, and a dredging operation to speed the flow of odorous effluent from a nearby paper mill. Currently two highways, an interchange, and an access road are under construction across the preserve. One of the utility easements will be increased in width eightfold. A pipe-line official recently commented to a Wildlife Preserves officer that this preserve was one of the best things that ever happened, for the land is kept open, acquisition is simplified, and land is cheap since it is not improved! As long as this attitude prevails our wetlands are doomed. But the question may well be asked: can Troy Meadows, considered one of the finest wetlands in the East, be saved or will these continuing encroachments destroy the values for which the area was preserved?

Pollution. Wetlands have long served as our reservoirs for human and industrial wastes. To these we have added pesticides, "waste" heat, and an increased flow of nutrients from agricultural lands. The effects have been to accelerate eutrophication, simplify species diversity, and exhaust the oxygen supply, leaving only anaerobic organisms. In the Hackensack meadows the tidal marshes are dominated by a single species, reed grass or *Phragmites*. Here it appears that the more diverse marsh flora has been eliminated by pollution. Although of minor value for water fowl, *Phragmites* still offers shelter and serves to catch sediments and minimize erosion.

Pesticides, especially insecticides, have markedly affected the ecology of wetlands. On Long Island, salt-marsh muds contain up to 32 pounds per acre of DDT following two decades of mosquito-control spraying. Biological magnification occurs at various trophic levels in the food chain from the phytoplankton through the sea birds, and levels appear sufficiently high in the marsh muds at this time to be subtly eliminating certain organisms (Woodwell, Wurster, and Isaacson 1967). Marine organisms, especially crustaceans, are extremely sensitive to the persistent pesticides. As little as 0.6 to 6 parts per *billion* will kill or immobilize a shrimp population in two days. A recent court case on Long Island has highlighted this environmental contamination by DDT and has led to a temporary injunction against the Suffolk County Mosquito Control Commission.

The osprey, closely associated with our coastal wetlands, has been rapidly declining in recent years. Here pesticides appear to be implicated. A study from marshes along the Connecticut River now reveals that only 0.5 young per nest are being reared, compared to the normal 2.5 young, and the eggs contain 5.1 ppm DDT. In Maryland, hatchability is slightly better—1.3 to 1.6 per nest—and DDT levels in the eggs are lower, only 3.0 ppm (Ames 1966).

Probably the most disturbing finding has been the report that DDT reduces photosynthesis in marine plankton (Wurster 1968). The ecological implications may be of major significance in modifying species diversity, in giving rise to explosive populations, and in aggravating already serious eutrophication. It may even result in subtle mortalities that might be difficult to determine by even the best sampling techniques.

NEED FOR A NATIONAL WETLAND SYSTEM

Private agencies such as the National Audubon Society, Nature Conservancy, Wildlife Preserves, Inc., Natural Areas Council, and Philadelphia Conservationists have all played a vital role in the preservation of such wetlands as Troy Meadows, the Tinicum Marshes in Philadelphia, and East River Marshes in Guilford, Connecticut. The preservation of the Great Swamp, New Jersey, although now under federal protection, was initially sparked by a group of private citizens.

At the municipal level we see Jamaica Bay, a famous 3,000-acre marsh and water complex, as part of the New York City Park System. And in Hempstead (Long Island), New York, 10,000 acres of tidal marshes owned by the town have been dedicated to wetland conservation through a joint program with the state. In the town of Woodbridge, Connecticut, there is zoning to prohibit the destruction of wetlands. Many towns have conservation commissions assisting in the preservation of the community's open-space resources, especially the wetlands. Land trusts are also being established, as in Guilford and Madison, Connecticut, where wetlands can be privately held or given to the town with certain legal restrictions.

Two states, Massachusetts and Rhode Island, have taken bold leadership in preserving tidal wetlands. The Massachusetts law prohibits dredging and filling the 45,000 acres remaining in Massachusetts. The Rhode Island law restricts use of coastal wetlands for the benefit of public health, marine fisheries, wildlife, and other conservation purposes. In New York the Long Island Wetland Bill provides funding up to 50 per cent of the total cost of development and 50 per cent of total cost of maintenance of town- or county-owned lands which have been dedicated for conservation purposes. Wetland legislation has been unsuccessful in Connecticut. However, Save the Wetlands Committee has a wetlands acquisition program under way.

At the federal level, estuarine legislation lately has authorized the Department of the Interior to inventory the nation's estuarine resources and set forth recommendations for a program of preservation. The Committee on Environmental Quality of the Federal Council on Science and Technology is currently considering means of resolving interagency conflicts in the use of the wetlands. Although there is a recognition of the problem, much bolder action is required if our wetland heritage is to be saved.

In conclusion, I should like to propose that we as a nation adopt a national wetlands policy. It is now recognized by economists that our productivity potential has reached such a level that the nation's economy and our high standard of living will not suffer by the preservation of such natural landscapes which will not only serve as an important natural resource but also will enhance the quality of life for all Americans (Krutilla 1968). Such a policy would give national recognition to the importance of wetlands. They would be inventoried and evaluated for the ecological role they serve, and vast acreages would be preserved in the national interest. Such a system might be patterned after the Wilderness system so that it could be defended against competitive land uses. This policy, we hope, would minimize conflicts of interest among government agencies and exercise certain controls over the private entrepreneur who may destroy for personal gain a resource of great value to the nation.

Until we have fully assessed these liquid assets, we will be unable to determine what is the desirable wetland mix that should receive permanent protection. With the possibility of our population doubling within the next forty years, this is the decade for action. For the urban environment it will mean increased open space and maximum habitat diversity, and it will assure a higher level of environmental quality in perpetuity.

REFERENCE

Ames, P. L. 1966. DDT residues in the eggs of the osprey in the northeastern United States and their relation to nesting success. *Jour. Appl. Ecol.* 3(Suppl.): 87–97.

Krutilla, J. V. 1968. Balancing extractive industries with wildlife habitat. Resources for the Future, Inc., Washington, D.C.

Niering, W. A. 1966. The life of the marsh: the North American wetlands. New York, McGraw-Hill Book Company, 232 pp.

U.S. Dept. of Interior. 1968. Man . . . an endangered species? Conservation Yearbook No. 4, 100 pp.

Woodwell, G. M., C. F. Wurster, and P. A. Isaacson, 1967. DDT residues in an east coast estuary: a case of biological concentration of a persistent insecticide. *Science* 156:821–824.

Wurster, C. F. 1968. DDT reduces photosynthesis by marine phytoplankton. *Science* 159:1474–1475.

Botanical gardens and horizons in algal research

SEYMOUR H. HUTNER

A botanical garden embedded in the northeast conurbation exemplifies the Antaeus effect. Hercules subdued this giant by holding him aloft, breaking his contact with the earth from which he drew his strength. Many an Antaean university department seeks its own downfall by suppressing organismal or "soft" biology in favor of "hard," or molecular biology. But a botanical garden retains the links to Earth needed for our urbanized society to stay vital and creative.

Yet, contemplation of flower beds and greenhouse exotica will hardly satisfy the new generation, far more steeped in science than bygone generations. Is it therefore appropriate for an institution like The New York Botanical Garden to support enterprises beyond the time-honored exhibits? I contend that such activity is needed lest our universities sink into a new sterile scholasticism or mandarinism, damaging the community which looks more than ever to universities for purpose and leadership. Interplay between garden and university is necessary for the health of both. I am familiar with algae and have dealt with

Reprinted from abridged version in *Garden Journal* 19(2): 37–40, 1969, entitled "The urban botanical garden: an academic wildlife preserve"; lightly edited.

flowering plants on one side and medical–veterinary problems on the other. A discussion of the place of algal research in our society, although obviously a limited subject, does permit a certain focus on these issues.

I conceive of The New York Botanical Garden as occupying part of the spiritual ecological niche in the New York megalopolis left vacant by the indifference of many universities and the lack of a land-grant university tradition in the area. This calls for some exposition.

The land-grant university, perhaps the most lasting contribution of the United States to civilization, is a symbiosis between university and community. In essence, the university pledges that it will address itself to the community's problems. The community (historically agricultural) pledges short-term support for trouble-shooters. But also, when the university judges that important problems can be solved only after substantial investments in fundamental research—necessarily coming from departments organized for both fundamentals and applications— the community will make this long-term investment without specifying how these fundamentals are to be quarried. The exceptions seem more ludicrous than serious, the famous one being the distaste of Wisconsin legislators for University of Wisconsin demonstrations of the virtues of oleomargarine.

This trust and intimacy between university and community has helped make the term "peasant" inappropriate in describing the heavily capitalized American farmers who grow most of our food. Land-grant universities, once derided as cow colleges, have largely avoided the perils of utilitarianism and babbittry on one hand, and on the other the kind of nineteenth-century Oxbridgian mandarinism that T. H. Huxley so fiercely opposed. The American egalitarianism did not permit the Germanic *geheimrat* system with its arrogant (but thorough!) scholarship to take root; likewise their Latin equivalents, the *catedráticos*, found few American counterparts.

Biology flourished, nourished from two sources: inquisitive farm boys and city boys frustrated for one reason or another in hopes of a medical career. But the molecular mandarins threaten to break the tacit land-grant compact and also to dry up the aforementioned sources of recruitment. This threatens perhaps the best hope for acquiring new purpose and spontaneity in our crowd-regimented lives. We are part of the transformation— slow but powerful—of ever-larger sectors of American life into a new pattern: the school or learning society. The university and kindred institutions such as botanical gardens become valuable fixed points in a dizzy world, and so new roles are thrust upon them.

I have been forced into these semi-cosmic reflections by the ways in which algae—obscure plants, the pets of hardly less obscure professors—became economically important and even glamorous.

Research on algae has contributed practical benefits to the community. Yet their study confronts man with questions about his deepest nature. This demands a restatement—and I hope my presumption will be forgiven—of T. H. Huxley's grand theme: "Man's place in nature" (Huxley 1959).

Man is an animal. Man and other animals probably came from photosynthetic plants. Zoology can be looked upon as a branch of plant pathology. As defined by Huxley, animals are those plant pests and predators that wander about in search of fuel and spare parts, preferably eaten in chunks. Perhaps the commonest animals on this planet are flagellates that are both photosynthetic and voracious. There may be more than 1,000 per milliliter in our coastal waters where the water is green with fish food, that is, plankton. The sluggishness of textbooks being what it is, these creatures are unmentioned or are dismissed in a few uneasy lines.

One of man's quests is to trace the origins of the physical basis of thought, molecule by molecule, for every function which makes man human. Consider vision: The light receptors for vision probably arose as light-sensitive carotenoids in photosynthetic bacteria, guiding them to light, then concentrated in the eyespot of algal flagellates. As Wolken (1967) has pointed out, these flagellates have a brain or a functional equivalent: they have something that transduces the light impulse into directed movement, and perhaps—who knows?—they have memory too, but experiments of requisite subtlety remain to be designed. Some flagellates, like man, require vitamin B_{12}. If blood from an anemia patient doesn't support *Euglena* growth, the anemia is the pernicious type. The industrial production of vitamin B_{12} is monitored with another plant-animal flagellate unknown in textbooks, and chicken is cheap thanks in part to supplementation of broiler mashes with B_{12}. Pernicious anemia can lead to brain and psychic deterioration; we again are back to the problem of the molecular origins of thought and personality.

The New York Botanical Garden through its director emeritus, Dr. William J. Robbins, now at The Rockefeller University, contributed to these enterprises. He was interested in plant growth and the evolution of its control. Here indeed is a confluence of farm-boy and medical motives. There are amusing byplays. Reasoning that if *Euglena* needed B_{12} in the laboratory, it must be getting it in nature, Drs. Robbins and Annette Hervey and Mary E. Stebbins (1950) measured the B_{12} in the fountain in front of the Museum building which then contained the laboratories; euglenas lived in that tiny pond the year around. Enough B_{12} was detected to support the euglenas. That petite pond became the prototype for investigations of the Big Pond; 70 per cent of the phytoplankton of the ocean—the grass of the sea— by present reckoning are B_{12} requirers. Part of the old textbook definition of plants as living in wholly mineral solutions went out the lab window, and a new chapter opened in oceanography and limnology. Here was a counterpart of William Blake's seeing the universe in a grain of sand and holding the universe in the palm of his hand.

Traffic jams have driven many affluent citizens to saltwater boating and fishing. In fishing off the New Jersey coast, they enact the American version of a British preoccupation: how is it that Thames sewage, after some magicking by North Sea plankton, returns, elegantly, as Dover sole, kippers, and jellied eels? Indeed, so efficient is this unpremeditated integration of sea farming with sewage disposal that, in a rare display of British braggadocio, I have heard worthies from Stevenage, their main sewage-research establishment, assert that every drop of London drinking water has, by conservative estimate, passed through at least seven kidneys. We in New York have not yet been pushed to this prodigy of technology, but the population pressure shows in another way: the need, created by intensive sport and commercial fishing, to maintain stocks of game fish off the coasts of New Jersey and Delaware despite vast fertilizations as the slow Labrador current sweeps the Hudson effluent towards Cape Hatteras. Hence the federal government has established a lab at Sandy Hook to develop methods of rearing marine game fish. Judging from Japanese experience, we suspect that larvae of marine fish will do best on a diet of tiny algal flagellates, perhaps mixed with diatoms, raised from pure cultures much as beer is brewed from initially pure cultures of yeast. Perhaps a larval tunicate or a crustacean stage must be interposed. These food flagellates, bearing such unfamiliar names as *Isochrysis* and *Monochrysis,* thus give rise to a new sort of industrial fermentation. Here is the beginning of modern sea farming in the United States. This technology, thanks to workers in the New Milford, Connecticut, shellfish lab, will permit reliable control of oyster rearing so that oysters can be cross-bred for flavor and disease resistance (Davis and Guillard 1958). Perhaps oysters will become again as accessible as chicken is now—once water pollution is checked.

Who are these algae and other phytoplankters at the base of the food pyramid? Can they be grown on a semi-industrial scale as food not only for game fish but also, as in the exciting pioneer experiments in Japan, for rearing shrimp, crabs, and abalone as well? The library resources of the Botanical Garden can assist in developing this agriculture.

The success of the land-grant idea inspires demand for "sea-grant" universities and, as Clark Kerr has said, for "urban-grant" universities to attack urban problems. But where are these biologists with vision—some call themselves ecologists—to come from?

I calculated some years ago that were everybody to do as the molecular biologists urged—to concentrate on *Escherichia coli* —it would soak up the world's supply of chemists, biologists, chemical engineers, and—oh unhappy day!—brewmasters, with nobody left over to solve the world's practical biological problems. And damned if the *New Scientist* two months ago didn't report that Francis Crick is promoting what sounds like an international *E. coli* year to solve this organism once and for all! The implication is that once *E. coli* is solved we shall have the skeleton key to the secret of life (Chedd 1968).

Now consider the urban student, parted from the rest of nature by the asphalt curtain. He wishes to understand life. Unlike the farm boy he is not familiar with the diversity of life. If not exactly handed a stone, he is handed a fractionation scheme for *E. coli* and a diagram of the postulated repression–expression mechanisms by which DNA somehow controls itself. Presumably any bright student can extrapolate the wiring diagram to his own brain.

How the student will occupy himself while this extrapolation is being made is *his* worry. I hear that in one school, the beginning student is fed a mixture of detailed diagrams of DNA sauced with these apocalyptic visions. Organisms come later as necessary evils—as unavoidable sources of these mechanisms. If, as noted, biologists were formerly recruited from farm boys and frustrated physicians, and if the molecular biologists had their way, biologists would have to come exclusively from mathematics and physics. The joke that Darwin could neither be admitted to nor survive in any up-and-coming American graduate school, because he couldn't meet the language and math requirements, acquires a dismal appositeness.

Let us begin to see new roles for an urban botanical garden withstanding the lust to cover the Earth with asphalt and concrete punctuated by parking meters: it is one seed-bed of coming American civilization. (I say "coming" in deference to my English friends.) We do not yet have in the United States the equivalent of the English cultivated amateur. Nor do we yet match the English in their passion for gardening, hiking, and erudite indoor pursuits. Nor are we like Israel a nation of archeologists. In our effluent society millions on vacation rove from motel to motel, from Howard Johnson to Howard Johnson, with a hasty visit to a national park perhaps sandwiched in between. There must be something better!

The intense biochemical professionalism of our university faculties ignores the fact that a new generation has arisen that will be able to take up scientific pursuits in its leisure time. Advent of the phase microscope, pre-mixed culture media, synthetic sea salts, screw-cap culture tubes, small efficient centrifuges, mail-order pressure cookers, and cheap fluorescent lighting make it possible even for apartment dwellers to take up the study of creatures of pond and ocean. The garden can serve as the source of information. If this sounds fanciful, let us recall that orchid rearing has come within the reach of the middle class now that the rearing of the delicate seedlings has become a routine microbiological procedure. One does not have to have the income of a Nero Wolfe to play with orchids at home. One does need a good library, however.

Eventually, professional societies, of protozoologists and algologists ("phycologists"), for example, must undertake the vast task of distilling their knowledge into a new kind of book—atlases and guides to the algae and protozoa, written comprehensibly for the informed amateur. I envision new kinds of coffee-table books, as beautiful as the art books that encumber the homes of our culture vultures (as passive culture consumers are now termed). But these new coffee-table books will be for use as well as enjoyment. (I plead guilty to being unable to altogether escape the Puritan ethic.) I contend that the goal of a professional scientific society rooted in natural history is to produce art: to depict the creatures and tell what they do. Scientific societies and institutions must be the new Medicis.

New ambitions emerge. An old one of mine is to trace the algae of the Hudson from its source in the pristine Lake Tear o' the Clouds high in the Adirondacks, where one would have to use a plankton net and centrifuge to concentrate the sparse micro-creatures; then down the Hudson in its mountain-brook stage, through the dairy lands north of Saratoga (the Hudson here receives an infusion of creamery wastes); then to the flat-lands where it amasses insults from the paper mills; then comes raw sewage from Troy and other downstream communities; then to Poughkeepsie where sea water is first encountered; then to that open septic tank called New York Harbor, where it receives everything from pastrami residues to ships' bilges; then out over the Hudson canyon and re-oxygenation by the marine plankton as the effluent joins the Labrador current. And then finally as striped bass off New Jersey.

Algae were studied by the undercapitalized professors of pre-vious generations. Consciously or not, they had taken vows of academic poverty and chastity (as good scholars they were short on obedience). I submit, therefore, that from the new class of cultivated amateur, backed by the competence and continuity of the Garden, will come many of the next generation of probers into man's nature. It may be that our particular kind of animals —the multicellular animals—originated in the brown-pigmented flagellates, perhaps very much like those used for rearing marine larvae. These flagellates are related to the brown seaweeds. The brown and red seaweeds have developed elaborate multicellular organization. What hormones coordinate their cells? Will these hormones hark back to the primordial origins of our hormones, or have they gone off on paths of their own?

Cancer is a disease of multicellularity. Most of these cellular regulators are still beyond experimental reach. We must explore even seaweeds for clues. And if we do not have a vital botanical garden and an informed community, again where will the scien-tists come from to attack the problems of man's nature and ecology?

An urban botanic garden, therefore, should be not only a botanical preserve; it should be a sort of academic wildlife pre-serve, a breeding ground for academics who from time to time will be exported to revitalize effete academic blood lines. These exports should be balanced by accession of rare academic fauna in danger of extinction, taxonomists or systematists, for example; it should also serve as an acclimatization way-station for introducing exotica such as physicists and chemists to the rigors of coping with the waywardness of uncentrifuged, unfractionated, almost unprogrammable living organisms.

REFERENCES

Chedd, G. 1968. EMBO [European Molecular Biology Organization]—the year of decision. [Interview with Dr. Max Perutz.] *New Scientist* (Feb. 29, 1968): 458–460.

An editorial insert boxed into this article includes this note: "*Project K*. The brainchild of Francis Crick, Project K takes its name from a particular strain, K_{12}, of the bacterium *Escherichia coli*. An all-out onslaught directed toward the *total* [*New Scientist*'s italics] understanding of the working of a single organism can now be contemplated for the first time. Because of the unity of biochemistry, such a complete understanding of one particular cell, even though it is a micro-organism, would throw a flood of light on the whole domain of cellular organization, including the economy and behavior of the human cell. The eventual rewards of such understanding would be the possibilities of practical control of cellular processes, with possible applications in medicine, in agriculture, and industry." [It is not clear whether this last sentence is a direct quotation, like the other quotation, from a formal proposal of EMBO's . . . "to the representatives of the European governments . . ."]

Davis, H. C., and R. R. Guillard. 1958. Relative value of ten genera of micro-organisms as foods for oyster and clam larvae. *Fishery Bull. Fish & Wildlife Service* 58 (136): 293–304.

Huxley, Thomas H. 1959. *Man's place in Nature*. Ann Arbor, Michigan, University of Michigan Press, AA–24, 184 pp.

Robbins, W. J., A. Hervey, and M. E. Stebbins. 1950. Studies on *Euglena* and vitamin B_{12}. *Bull. Torrey Bot. Club* 77: 423–441.

Wolken, J. J. 1967. *The biology of Euglena*, 2nd edition. New York, Appleton-Century-Crofts, 204 pp.

CHALLENGE FOR SURVIVAL *Commentary*

by Edmund M. Fenner

Instead of commenting directly on Dr. Hutner's paper, I am going to follow an alternate suggestion to discuss industry's efforts in water-pollution control.

Despite what I am sure many of you believe, despite what you read, despite what you hear, much of industry today is working diligently to improve water quality. I don't mean to imply that the job is nearly done, for such is far from true. Much effort, time, and money must still be expended before control is achieved.

To illustrate industry's present efforts, I would like to tell you what my company, Johns-Manville, is doing to eliminate the water pollution created by its production operations.

Before doing so, however, I would like to describe briefly how we have organized our company to tackle all our environmental problems. Our system is nearly unique in industry. We call it the "Total-Environment" approach. It is a coordinated effort to improve working and community environments; to provide health protection and safety for employees and customers; to control the quality of the air and water used and shared with neighbors. The unique element is that all these varied efforts are coordinated by a single, central agency: our Department of Environmental Control.

The word environment, as used in our definition of this department's function, identifies three distinct and different fields of concern:

Occupational environment. The working conditions inside our plants that could affect the health, safety, and welfare of our 22,000 employees.

Community environment. The external conditions created by our operations that could affect the health and welfare of the communities around our fifty-four manufacturing locations. This, of course, refers to both air and water pollution and therefore relates directly to this symposium.

Product toxicology. If some of our products present a potential health hazard to the user, then we ensure that our customers are aware of the situation and are instructed in the proper method of handling the product.

It is my responsibility, as Director of the department, to co-ordinate and administer our corporate programs and activities for environmental control in all three fields. Now, for the specifics of water-pollution control.

Johns-Manville has ten divisions operating seventeen distinctly different manufacturing processes at fifty-four locations in the United States and Canada. Eleven of these seventeen manufacturing processes could create water pollution. Thirty-eight of our plants utilize one or more of these pollution-causing processes. Twenty of the thirty-eight have no problem because of existing satisfactory effluent disposal procedures. What of the other eighteen plants where pollution could and does exist? Let me review our program.

Even with our variety of manufacturing processes that could create pollution, we have adopted one basic approach toward correction of our present problems. This approach is very simply expressed in the words "water conservation." By this I mean the close-up of our manufacturing processes through re-circulation and re-use of water, resulting either in the elimination of effluent or in the minimal discharge of clean effluent. Elimination of pollution by water conservation, although easy to talk about, will be difficult and costly to obtain. We intend to do it.

I mentioned eighteen plants with actual or potential water-pollution problems. We have one plant with a new closed system that has solved its problem. We have six plants where a problem presently exists. Close-up re-circulation systems have already been engineered, and funds provided. The installation of equipment is under way. Pollution elimination in these plants will be accomplished during 1968. We have eleven plants where pollution might become worrisome. Here engineering studies are underway to determine the best methods and costs for correction.

That is a brief look at our program to eliminate the water-pollution problems caused by our operations. In closing I would like to add that industry as a whole is making considerable effort to achieve water-pollution control. These efforts are showing results. However, complete control will take a great deal of time, money, research, and dedication. I am firmly convinced that industry will accept this challenge and do its full share to assure our survival.

Survival of plants and man

LEWIS MUMFORD

Though I have on two or three other occasions been given the task of summarizing a conference, it always turns out that the job is beyond my powers, indeed possibly beyond anyone's powers, and that the main effect of our discussions is to point to the necessity of holding still another conference, to bring to a sharper focus the ideas we have been putting forth and probing. But since I have been listening assiduously to the many able papers that have been presented during the last two days, I could not help assembling my own general impression of the results. And with all respect to both the speakers and the audience, I must say that, although a great amount of important information has been conveyed to us, we have only been delicately nibbling at the edges of the problem—the challenge of survival, for men and plants.

If I venture to speak very frankly, without the usual degree of scientific detachment, it is because I am in fact not a scientist but a Dutchess County gardener: my sole qualification here is that I have handled plants, have assisted in a modest way in their growth, and have learned something about the nature of life, including my own, by observing how selective, how self-respecting, how wilful, indeed choosey, plants can be, in singling out the

Reprinted from *Garden Journal* 18(3): 66–71, 1968; lightly edited.

conditions necessary for their survival, and still more, for their fullest growth and flowering.

One of the things that has struck me about this conference is that so little mention has been made of the plants themselves and the great part they have played in encouraging man's own development; and further how essential it now is to reclaim and extend the dominion of plants once more, if man's own survival is to be secured. Though not a few references have been made to primeval forms, like the algae, I propose to widen our area of exploration sufficiently to take in the whole world of living plants, and to suggest that the chances of our own survival are closely bound up with the recovery of the common territory we have too readily surrendered to an underdimensioned, organically deficient technology, now producing a multitude of environmental changes that are undermining the very existence of both plants and men.

So let me ask you, first of all, what will be left of the plant world if we allow the basically village culture, founded on a close symbiotic partnership between man and plants, to disappear? For some twelve thousand years, all the higher achievements of civilization have rested on this culture, one devoted to the constructive improvement of the habitat and the loving care of plants—their selection, their nurture, their breeding, their enjoyment. That culture, as Edgar Anderson suggested, originally made some of its best discoveries in breeding by being equally concerned with the color, the odor, the taste, the flower and leaf patterns, the sexual functions, and the nutritive qualities of plants, valuing them not only for food and medicine, but for esthetic delight. There are plenty of people working in scientific laboratories today who, though they may still call themselves biologists, have no knowledge of this culture, except by vague hearsay, and no respect for its achievements. They dream of a world composed mainly of synthetics and plastics, in which no creatures above the rank of algae or yeasts would be encouraged to grow.

In the earlier stages of human development, the relationship between man and plants had been a one-sided one, not an active partnership. Though plants, birds, and insects have always been among man's chief foods, man was able to do very little to modify natural vegetation, still less to assist in the cultivation of favored plants: man's relation to the existing botanical system was parasitic rather than symbiotic. But first by preservation and selection, and then by active cultivation, man found himself, once the last glacial period came to an end, able actively to reshape his habitat and to do something for the plant world. In doing so, he made his own environment immensely more habitable, more edible, and—what is equally important—more lovable. And in the very act of establishing a new role for plants, man both deepened his roots in the landscape and gave himself a new leisure and a new security. It was in the garden that man, thanks largely to woman's efforts, for the first time felt completely at home.

In my recent book, *The Myth of the Machine*, I pointed out that the great advances in neolithic domestication were made with hardly any mechanical aids. One of man's instruments, fire, had been in his hands for some 500 thousand years. The other was the stone ax, with which man could chop down trees. Those who equate neolithic plant domestication with grain cultivation and plow culture have not caught up with recent archaeology; for though these last inventions were extremely important, the major advances of the neolithic revolution had been made long before through a fuller understanding of plant nurture, plant selection, plant hybridization, in the timing of cultivation to fit the seasons, and in the close watching of the relation of plant growth to soil, water, ash, and dung.

With the aid of the ax, neolithic man opened up clearings in the forests of the highlands where the plants he chose would have sufficient space, moisture, nutriment, and freedom from competition to thrive, while on the edge of the clearings in the same area the berry bushes took hold and spread about further through the cooperation of the greedy finches and cardinals. This picture of the beginnings of neolithic domestication—though of course partly hypothetic—corresponds to the growing archaeological evidence, and emphasizes something that needs emphasis, namely, that though grain cultivation capped this process, what was even more important for human development was the combination of plant variety, continuity of occupation, and the growing inter-dependence of man, plants, insects, and birds. Up to this point man's greatest improvements had been made with the materials of his own body: the symbols of dream, ritual, language, and art. Now he was at least sufficiently well established to enter into an active partnership with plants, and later with the animals that paleolithic hunters had venerated. With plant domestication, man's inner life and his outer life achieved a balance.

This active partnership between man and plants did something more than ensure their common survival: it provided, as never before, the conditions for their further development. Every domesticated plant and animal we use today, with a few trifling exceptions like the boysenberry and the coffee plant, was orig-inally a product of neolithic domestication, whose clearings and tilled acres and vineyards and orchards finally engirdled the Earth. Though the period of botanical and agricultural experi-ment came to a climax before the Bronze Age, this culture has a record of longevity and continuity that indicates how admirably it met the conditions necessary for both ecological balance and human development in every kind of geographic environment. The local center of this culture was the successor of the neolithic village, where the traditional rites, the traditional customs, the traditional lore of cultivation, were passed on from generation to generation, from century to century: slowly absorbing the im-provements introduced by the higher cultures, being guided by the new astronomical calendar, making use of the horse and the ox and the plow, gratefully accepting the iron hoe and the iron spade, yet always stable enough to pass on the essential knowl-edge of plant needs and cultivation processes and human pur-poses to ensure the village's survival. If survival were to be our only criterion of fitness, this basic neolithic culture would hold the record. That village economy spread over the entire planet and it left everywhere the imprint of its essential features:

variety, balance, controlled and limited growth. Until the present generation, four-fifths of the human race, according to the French geographer Max Sorre, lived in villages that were closer in every aspect to the neolithic community than to any contemporary metropolitan complex. If this culture never reached the constructive heights of the urban civilization of the Bronze, the Iron, or the Nuclear Age, it never descended to their depths of destruction and extermination.

Both plants and men—even when due allowance is made for overbrowsed forests and overgrazed pastures and eroded hillsides—were safe in the hands of such backward communities: their very feebleness and lethargy were an insurance against gross human mismanagement. But all this has changed, almost within our own generation; and the ancient symbiotic relation, so helpful to both human and plant life, may be dissolved in an excess of technological dynamism, within our life-time.

Those who still talk glibly about the inevitability of further mechanization and urbanization, who look forward to an almost solid urbanoid mass sometimes called Megalopolis, reaching from Maine to Florida, or even covering the greater part of the planet, do not in the least realize the implications of their complacent predictions. With almost criminal levity, they have accepted, as if it were a fatal necessity, the ruthless destruction of the balanced environment essential to human life. On a purely physical level, that balance is dependent upon the part played by plants in maintaining the oxygen-nitrogen cycle necessary to plant, animal, and above all human existence. For twelve thousand years agriculture, as practiced by village communities, ensured human continuity. Today the villages are being wiped out, the farming population reduced in the United States to a mere tenth of the total; and precisely the richest soils and the most cultivable areas are being made into urban deserts.

I have no wish to frighten you; but it is time we realized, if all too belatedly, that this lopsided technology has little prospect, if it goes on expanding at its present rate, of surviving for even a century, much less twelve thousand years. As the cultivated areas shrink, as millions of square miles of good soils are turned into sterile expressways, concrete clover-leaves, parking lots, and airports; as the air, the water, and the soil become polluted with chemical poisons, nuclear wastes, and inorganic debris; as essential bird and insect species die off, the prospects of human survival on any terms diminish.

As long as from seventy to ninety per cent of the world's population was engaged in cultivating plants, human life as a whole was secure. In the past century this biological factor of safety has shrunk. Tomorrow it may be gone. If our leaders were sufficiently awake to these dangers they would plan not for urbanization but for ruralization.

Our present dangerous lack of ecological balance is largely due to the fact that our technology, in overcoming our organic limitations and increasing, by an enormous factor, the amount of energy at our disposal, has none of the self-limiting and self-correcting devices that organic systems have developed. Some of you perhaps remember the illustration W. H. Hudson gave in *Far Away and Long Ago* of what happened on the pampas of the Argentine when a single plant, the Canada thistle, invaded this environment. Within a short time the herds of cattle were starving and the economy was threatened, because the thistles, freed from the restraints of their original environment, grew higher than a horse's head, and became so thick that cattle could not make their way through them.

Well, modern technology, whether under capitalist or communist exploitation, has proved to be the Canada thistle of our culture. The aim of our technology is not to enhance life and to foster the processes of growth and efflorescence, but to exploit power and bring ever larger portions of the environment, and of human life, too, under more and more rigid and regimented modes of control. Expansion, magnification, multiplication, quantification, speed, turnover, profit, "overkill"—these are the criteria of technical success. In the interests of an expanding economy, we have been settling for a contracted life in which no organic function will be tolerated unless it can be profitably attached to some corporate megamachine and made to conform to its requirements.

But why should we regard our machines as more sacred than organisms and treat their needs as superior to those of animals and plants and men? Why should our economy seek to expand every year, instead of aiming, like organic systems, at establishing a balance favorable to human needs in the order of their biological and social importance? Why should we allow ourselves to be assaulted, for example, with supersonic transportation, when the hours saved for the passengers on these planes will be offset by the days lost to millions of groundlings whose lives will be periodically shattered by the noise of their breaking the sound barrier? Does man live by transportation alone?

A colleague of mine, a professor at M.I.T., has calculated that if a superjet plane, in a single flight over a population of as little as five million people, disturbed the life of each one for only ten seconds, the amount of time lost on the ground would add up to something like 13,800 hours. In all, a total of 578 man-days would be lost in order to enable a few score high-pressured travelers to reach their destination a few hours sooner. Such fake time saving would be laughed out of existence were it not for the fact that our machine worship has become as fantastically irrational as the star worship of the Aztecs, who slaughtered thousands of lives every year as a religious sacrifice.

This same system of jet propulsion has now been applied, at least in military models, to land transportation in vehicles without wheels; and Marshall McLuhan has even proclaimed that both the wheel and the roadway have become obsolete and all transportation would be conducted on a cushion of air. Apparently Professor McLuhan has not yet learned that the exhausts of ordinary motor cars and jet engines have already risen to a dangerous level; and that anything like a universal transportation system by jets would soon reach an extermination level. Even the most vaporous mind should by now be sufficiently familiar with the scientific data to realize that such a system of transportation, operated on a large scale, would be an invitation to mass suicide.

The notion that our age has an obligation to foster such technological depredations in the name of progress must be challenged. Whose progress—man's or the machine's? Why indeed should any government subsidize jet-age travel when the net effect is to ruin every landscape and every historic site to which we bring our jet liners and motor coaches? Until now Delphi, for instance, presented one of the most wonderful landscapes in the world: a landscape whose profound religious atmosphere remained, though the temples are ruined and the religion itself has passed away. But, speaking for myself, I don't dare go back to Delphi. I know that it has already become a parking lot, and in a few years all that made it so precious will, if our present habits continue, disappear: even the eagles will probably cease to hover in the sky, and the sea of olive trees in the Vale of Amphissa will be cut down to make way for hotel sites and golf courses.

Isn't it time for us to ask ourselves a few serious questions about the overheated technology upon which we have become so dependent, and the expanding economy that we have been so sedulously promoting and coddling, at the expense of organic balance and development, to say nothing of human health, poise, sanity? We are no longer in control of this overpowered and overpowering corporate mechanism: we are driving this supposedly up-to-date vehicle without either a steering wheel or a brake, and our only form of control is through the use of an accelerator to make it go faster, even though that greatly increases the danger.

Our Canada thistle technics has the effect of reducing all life to the level of the machine, even as it reduces all human intelligence to the level of a computer, without the feelings, emotions, purposes, desires, hopes that bring us into relation with the lives of other men and indeed with the whole cosmos of living beings. We are creating a monoculture which is becoming more standardized, more homogenized and flattened out every day. Even our recreation is no longer the sphere of spontaneity and self expression: it too has become standardized; and in many of our overcrowded national parks in summer, the smog and the rubbish and the defacement of the landscape fully equal that produced in our cities. Is it not significant that even on the open water speed alone has become the criterion of enjoyment? The fast-moving, noisy, air-polluting motorboat has taken the place of the more adventurous sailboat, which called for muscular exercise, a weather eye, a knowledge of sea and shore, along with self-confidence, even courage.

In the course of our meetings we have been examining, in a shy, somewhat circuitous way, some of the effects of this humanly deficient monoculture, with its insidious displacement of human needs, its erosion and pollution of the natural environment, and its reduction of the area of both wild and cultivated lands. What we must realize is the fact that though science and technology have brought mankind huge benefits, which we have every right to be proud of and every reason to enjoy, they have also burdened us with painful deficits that must be liquidated, and they threaten us with serious disorders that we must promptly cope with. What is worse, these negative results are in part due to the very superabundance of their products, like the cans and bottles that now litter our roadsides, so-called disposable containers that no one has yet found an economic and decent way of disposing of.

If we are to recover both our ecological and our cultural balance, we must subject our entire economy to a rigorous examination, and deal with our difficulties at their source, instead of paying attention to them only when they have become so embedded in the whole structure of production and consumption that they cannot be removed except with heroic exertions and at extravagant cost. In other words, instead of becoming heartsick over our littered roadsides, our rubbish dumps, our auto cemeteries, we must challenge the whole economy of the disposable container. Instead of just fighting against turning our last wetlands into jet ports, we must challenge the notion that all other human needs should be sacrificed to fast transportation. In short, we must dare to question the religion of the machine, and be ready to flout the superstitious observances and taboos that have been erected to ensure the supremacy of automation, computerism, and electronic communication over more important services to human life that the wilderness areas, the cultivated farmland and parkland, vineyards and orchards produce.

If we intend to provide for the survival of plants and men, we had better become iconoclasts of this machine-centered religion: we must throw down these idols, and ask the bat-eyed priests of technology what on earth they think they are doing. Obviously, the Earth, in all its variety and complexity of environments, is the last place for which they feel any sense of responsibility: they are off on dizzy trips to outer space—"trips" in *both* present senses of the word. One of the high priests of this religion, Buckminster Fuller, has even said, seemingly with a straight face, that the space capsule is the one truly perfect environment yet invented by man; and it is increasingly plain that the chief end of this religion is to reduce the Earth itself to a space capsule: the most deadly, defunctionalized, dehumanized environment that the mind of man has yet conceived—compared to which the most backward neolithic mud village was a paradise of creativity and human autonomy.

Instead of defending our position, putting up a dreary rearguard fight against the armies that are conquering the Earth for the sake of unlimited power and profit and prestige, the time has come for man and his plants to join forces in a counterattack. Mere survival is not good enough: we must devise a strategy to ensure the further development of plants and men. The odds against our success are far from hopeless, for in fact, all life is on our side—and has been since the very beginning, slow though we have been to realize this fact. Here I return to my original theme: we have something to learn from the plants. The flowering plants, above all, have much to teach us about our own nature. Not by accident, the young, who are in revolt against our power-stricken and machine-regimented society, have seized upon the symbolism of the flower, and call themselves "flower children." In a very innocent, simpleminded, sometimes downright silly way, they have used the flower symbol to express their rejection of this automated and computerized and life-hostile technology. We, too, must learn to be flower children again, and rejoin the old procession and pageant of life.

Yes: the plants, above all the flowering plants, have something to teach us. Remember Loren Eiseley's beautiful chapter in *The Immense Journey*, about that turning point in organic development when the Age of Reptiles gave way to the Age of Mammals, those warm-blooded beasts that suckled their young. Eiseley pointed out that the Age of Mammals was accompanied by an explosion of flowers; and that the reproductive system of the angiosperms was responsible, not merely for covering the whole earth with a green carpet composed of many different species of grass—over four thousand—but for intensifying vital activity of every kind, since the nectars and pollens and seeds and fruits and the succulent leaves dilated the senses, exhilarated the mind, and immensely increased the total food supply. Not merely was this explosion of flowers a cunning device of reproduction, but the flowers themselves assumed a variety of forms and colors that in most cases cannot possibly be accounted for as having survival value in the struggle for existence. It may add to the attraction of a lily's sexuality to have all of its sexual organs displayed amid teasingly open petals; but the huge success of so many Compositae, with their insignificant florets, shows that biological prosperity might have been purchased without any such floral richness and inventiveness.

Efflorescence is an example of nature's untrammeled creativity and the fact that floral beauty cannot be explained or justified on purely utilitarian grounds is precisely what makes this explosion so wonderful—and so typical of all life processes. Biological creativity exists for its own sake: if survival were all that mattered, life might have remained in the primal ooze, or crept no further upward than the lichens. The capacity for self-transformation has not yet been expressed in any currently accepted biological doctrine, nor yet is it explained by the chemical instrumentality of DNA. But long before man himself became conscious of beauty, beauty existed in the endlessly varied forms and colors of the flowering plants. The selection and encouragement of these plants, quite apart from any utilitarian value, was what gave man his first real glimpse, perhaps, of paradise—for paradise is only the original Persian name for a walled garden. The capacity for exuberant expression symbolized by efflorescence—this is the primal gift of life; and to consciously maintain it and guard it and expand it is one of the ultimate reasons for human existence. There are no mechanical or electronic substitutes for this kind of creativity.

But observe: our present-day civilization, in allowing its neolithic foundations to crumble, now finds itself in a curious position. Thanks to man's superb intelligence and his ability to translate mathematical and physical abstractions into practical inventions, the gift of exuberance has been transferred from the world of living organisms to the world of machines, electronic apparatus, and power utilities. Here we are deliberately displacing organic variety and replacing it with a more limited mechanical variety. Ulysses Hedrick tells us that over ninety species of apples were cultivated in America before 1860, while today, to judge by the supermarkets, there are only two varieties left: Delicious and McIntosh. Yet at the same time there has been an explosion of machines, for the technological world shows immense vitality and exuberance that threatens to suppress every other manifestation of life. The most dynamic parts of this technology, so far from being devoted to the cultivation of plants or the culture of human beings, derive from our massive preparations for war; and in their actual use they display a callous indifference, indeed a stupendous and stultifying hostility, to the needs of organisms.

In *The Myth of the Machine* I have drawn a parallel between the high-powered technology of the Pyramid Age, which produced the towered cities, the great canal systems, dams, irrigation works, and along with these, war and destruction on an unparalleled scale, and the megatechnic organizations of our own time. In both examples, the engineering was magnificent: don't think I undervalue the technical achievement. But it was the lack of ecological insight that resulted, in Sumer, not merely in the silting up of the canals but in the salinization of the fields and in the eventual ruin of agriculture. Something of the same nature is happening in the United States today.

As if the lethal smog from our multimillion cars and factory chimneys were not a sufficient threat to life, we extend the area of poisoning by spraying pesticides and herbicides recklessly over the landscape, and by pouring detergents into already heavily polluted streams. The birds and the insects now exist in ever-dwindling numbers, thanks largely to DDT—a nerve poison whose use should never have been permitted—and the vegetables and flowers and fruits dependent upon their cooperation in fertilization will, if this process goes on, be doomed. Hence the morbid interest some biologists have shown in developing sub-foods, from algae and yeasts. But the full meaning of this attack upon every mode of life by our war-directed technology has hardly yet been grasped. What it means, at bottom, is that we are regressing from the age of mammals, birds, and flowers, back to the age of the cold-blooded reptiles.

Before we let the armored reptiles and the flying reptiles reconquer the planet, we had better take a good hard look at the kind of existence that is now offered to us as the highest expression of our scientific age. Why should we offer homage to machines, as if they were superior kinds of organisms, and think so humbly and distrustfully about the human mind, with its incalculable reserves of potential creativity, provided it keeps hold of our historic nature and in touch with all its cooperating resources in the living environment. Why should we accept the notion of an expanding economy as a method of salvation, when actually what we need is a *balanced* economy, which will put the needs of life before the claims of profit, prestige, or power. Why should we waste our surplus on mechanical gadgets and inane superfluities, when we might be cultivating our gardens and bringing forth new plants—some if possible with a higher protein content!—that we never cultivated before. Why should we invest public funds in sterile highrise tenements, in all their dreary uniformity, when the environment of life demands homes, gardens, communities that express individuality and identity, as every natural species does, as a condition for normal development. Why, to put it briefly, should we value parking lots above parks, and content ourselves with plastic flowers, mockeries of both nature and art, fit only to be placed, Nazi-fashion, at the entrance to extermination camps. Every city should be a garden city, for gardens can give more intense sensory awakening and delight than any noxious halucinogen.

These are not private questions or peculiar answers. The young are already asking them. If we had not shut our minds to feedback, we should all of us have been asking them long ago. It is incredible that it was only in 1938 that Landsberg wrote about Air Pollution, and no one else had taken the subject seriously, except in terms of dirt, though as Landsberg wisely pointed out, the smoke nuisance was the subject of a constructive paper by John Evelyn three whole centuries ago. Yet it is more absurd to tolerate a technology producing high-speed changes on a worldwide scale, but with no apparatus for detecting its errors, no effective public method for correcting them, and no willingness to utilize the scientific information available if this threatens to limit its continued expansion and profit making. The Romans, in their high regard for justice, used to say "Let justice prevail, though the ceiling fall." But our technocrats are so committed to the worship of the sacred cow of technology that they say in effect: Let the machine prevail, though the earth be poisoned, the air be polluted, the food and water be contaminated, and mankind itself be condemned to a dreary and useless life, on a planet no more fit to support life than the sterile surface of the moon.

It is against this miscarriage of science and technology, this wholesale curtailment of the possibilities of life, this continued threat of collective extermination by nuclear bombardment that might wipe out all higher life on this planet, or by slower but equally deadly modes of poisoning, that the young today are in revolt. In their use of the flower as the symbol of vitality and creativity, of unashamed sexuality and love, they are reminding us of the terms upon which men and plants have not only survived but prospered together—with the aid, of course, of all the other species and orders whose combined activities have produced a living environment. Unless we change our minds, as the young are doing, and alter our whole routine of living, we shall not need a nuclear war to bring the whole evolutionary process to a halt. So my final word to you is to remember what the young are saying to us, in words that were first used by John Ruskin: "There is no wealth but life." Let it flower!

Date Due

Demco 38-297